IN CU

A COMPANION TO ST UM

by

RUDOLPH KENNA

and

IAN SUTHERLAND

STRATHCLYDE
POLICE

in association with

GLASGOW G3 7EH
0141-429 3479

First Published 1998
ISBN: 0 952947 13 7

CONTENTS

AUTHORS' PREFACE

STRATHCLYDE Police Museum has amassed its collection during the past 200 years in which a developing police service has operated in the West of Scotland. The collection is a colourful and developing reminder of policing's complex but intimate relationships with society. Police officers are publicly visible and always accountable reflections of society's need for safety, order and justice. Police officers of all ranks work - often alone - at the interface between those concepts.

That can be dangerous and controversial. Mistakes have been made and will continue to be made. Equally, the work of police officers is regularly praised by press, politicians and public.

Policing reflects public agendas - pre-occupation with alcohol in all its aspects in the 19th century, for example, or narcotic and hallucinogenic drugs in the 20th century.

But, as the collection at Pitt Street reveals, there is a policing agenda, too. A deeply held ethic of public service is reflected in the number of officers who have died on duty, or who volunteered for both World Wars. However imperfectly expressed on occasion, for example, in the case of Oscar Slater in 1909, there is a belief in justice as a concept which applies to all citizens regardless of origin, class or belief. Police officers are "citizens in uniform" - responsible ultimately to elected representatives of the public. In the final analysis, they do what the public asks them to do.

Much of that story is about democracy and political rights. Policing in early 19th century Scotland stemmed primarily from localised initiatives, under which the nation's rapidly growing burghs obtained private Police Acts. Glasgow obtained its legislation in 1800, Edinburgh in 1805, Paisley in 1806, Greenock in 1810 and Dundee in 1824.

First public enactment regulating police forces came into force in 1833. That was merely an enabling Act, and of 183 burghs eligible to adopt its provisions, only 12 embraced the legislation in its entirety by 1847.

Growth of police forces under private Police Acts was part of the evolution of local democracy. In the early 19th century, most burghs were controlled by self-perpetuating oligarchies. Urban bourgeoisie and professional people had little access to political power until the Scottish Reform Act of 1833. Thereafter, town councils were firmly in the hands of the bourgeoisie. Between 1800 and 1830, when yet unreformed burghs began to create police forces, oligarchs were compelled to negotiate with the prosperous - if politically feeble - middle classes. It was they would have to pay assessments to support new police forces.

The rising bourgeoisie insisted on election of police commissioners administering private Police Acts. In Glasgow and Edinburgh, police elections were limited to those paying house rentals of £10 or more per annum. But Aberdeen and Paisley opted for a £5 franchise and, briefly, Dundee had a £2 franchise.

These arrangements were remarkably democratic for their time. They preceded the great Reform Acts of 1832 and 1833, which extended the franchise to £10 householders.

1

In 1856, Sir Henry Cockburn remarked: "The gradual extension of the police system over our towns trained the people to expect and to exercise the elective privilege."

By 1852, 67 Scottish burghs had police forces - comprising 1370 officers. No fewer than 46 of those "forces" had complements of three officers - or less. Glasgow mustered 613 officers, Edinburgh 318 and Dundee 66.

In the wake of clearances and famine, Highland migrants and Irish immigrants - most of them in desperate straits - roamed the countryside or headed for towns. Such vagrants might have become burdens on rural parishes. Under Scotland's Poor Law, three years' residence in a parish qualified a person for relief - regardless of parish of origin. Early rural police forces were established on "vagrancy routes" to major cities. Rural officers "excluded" potentially costly vagrants or moved them into adjacent counties. NIMBY has a long history.

Farrmers feared that potatoes and other crops might be grubbed up by starving vagrants en route to industrialising towns. Rural authorities assumed connections between vagrancy and crime. Creation of police forces was a response to that perception.

Arrival in rural Scotland of large numbers of railway navvies also accelerated formal policing. Navvies - "industrial gypsies" - lived in townships of crude bothies. Violence flared easily in such encampments - fuelled by cheap raw spirits. Pay days resulted in wild disorder. Fugitive criminals often took refuge in navvy settlements. An Act of 1857 compelled Scottish counties to establish police forces.

In the last four decades of the 19th century, many burgh forces merged with county forces. By the end of the 19th century, Scotland was well on the way to becoming a recognisably policed society in the modern sense. Both burghs and counties had forces capable of co-operation and rapid concentration in times of emergency.

Amalgamations quickened in the 20th century - driven by social changes and tensions, fast-developing technology, growth of motor transport and the effects of political reforms such as regionalisation. Strathclyde Police Museum reflects that process, too. In the late-20th century, rapid changes are again affecting society - and will inevitably affect policing.

There has been talk of the formation of a "Royal Scottish Police" operating on a Scotland-wide basis, under devolution arrangements in the 21st century. Policing is increasingly international, too. And aspects of Scottish policing have found their way into international expression. "Diced caps" - the so-called "Sillitoe Tartan" - believed to have been introduced by Glasgow chief constable Percy Sillitoe in the 1930s are rapidly being adopted by police forces throughout the world.

Policing in the West of Scotland gained its spurs - and the beginnings of public respect - in dealing with Chartist riots in the 1840s. Most of those events were intensely localised. They were also part of a national and international movement - leading to the emergence of citizenship in democratic societies.

Strathclyde Police Museum is also a museum of public issues and progress. The West of Scotland's "citizens in uniform" would have it no other way. ❑

2

"GRUB FIRST, MORALS LATER!"

S TRATHCLYDE Police Museum features a display centring on an officer wearing an 1847 uniform. In the early 19th century, such officers faced the angry consequences of widespread unemployment and hardship in the West of Scotland.

Following the Napoleonic Wars, food prices rose sharply, income tax was abolished - and indirect taxation on tea, tobacco, spirits, and other commodities hit the poor hardest.

Handloom weavers faced drastic falls in earnings caused by competition from power loom factories. They became easy prey to social unrest. Hard-line employers resisted embryo trade unionism.

In 1810, "persons connected with a combination lately discovered to exist among journeymen cotton spinners" attacked the house of a Glasgow mill-owner. In 1816, workers rioted in Calton, Glasgow. A soup kitchen was attacked, along with a "steam loom" factory. Cavalry were sent in. Councillors took palliative action: starving weavers were employed on levelling Glasgow Green.

In 1819, unemployed weavers assembled on Glasgow Green, demanding action to alleviate distress. During similar disturbances in Paisley, the Riot Act was read four times in five days - a Scottish record.

Rioters in Bridgeton, Glasgow, smashed windows and attacked JPs and special constables. Jobless weavers also rioted in Stonehouse, Lanarkshire. In Airdrie, a mob prevented swearing-in of special constables.

A mass meeting in Glasgow protested at the notorious "Peterloo Massacre" in Manchester. Influential citizens became alarmed. There was little faith in the capacity of the city's tiny police force to handle serious unrest. Wealthy citizens raised a volunteer force of "Glasgow Sharpshooters".

In 1820, police and soldiers arrested 27 "radical delegates" at a house in Gallowgate, Glasgow. The men were said to represent groups in Strathaven, Airdrie, Kirkintilloch, Paisley, Elderslie, and Ayr. *The Herald* reported:

"The military guard in returning to barracks was followed by a crowd of disorderly persons, and assaulted with stones. Four of the most active in the mob were laid hold of, and are in custody. A precognition is going on with a view to their trial for this offence, which has of late become very common, and requires to be put down by the interference of the civil power. Sentinels at the jail were doubled, and in a short time the city attained its usual tranquillity."

A Glasgow-based radical paper, *The Spirit of the Union*, circulated as far as Ayr. Its editor was convicted of sedition and transported for five years. Radicals were arrested throughout Ayrshire - for allegedly "inciting operatives to desist from work". Mauchline

3

was said to have harboured "a committee of radicals".

In Glasgow, cotton employers offered 300 guineas' reward for information on an "armed gang of ruffians" who fired several shots into a Bridgeton house occupied by working mill employees. An attempt was made to burn a Milngavie mill, using tallow, tar and gunpowder.

Handloom weavers were largely self-educated - many influenced by dissident writers such as Thomas Paine. As early as 1787, a group of Calton weavers, rioting in protest against severe wage reductions, were fired on by soldiers. Three were killed, three others mortally wounded. More than 6000 sympathisers attended the funerals at Calton burying ground.

There were reports of radicals drilling in secret. Meetings of more than 50 persons were banned. On April 2, 1820, a "proclamation" declared a "Provisional Government of Scotland". There have been allegations that this was the work of *agents provocateur.* Weavers from Parkhead, Glasgow, were among the ringleaders.

On April 4, 1820, most millworkers in Glasgow and Paisley were on strike. On April 5, radicals, mainly weavers, met on Glasgow Green, and set out for Falkirk, hoping to seize the Carron Iron Works, Scotland's cannon foundry. En route, they were joined by weavers from outlying villages - and were put to flight at Bonniemuir, near Castlecary.

A group of Strathaven weavers, marching to Glasgow, reached the rallying point of Cathkin Braes only to find it deserted. Most were arrested while returning to their homes. As late as April 7, a body of Bridgeton weavers made for Kirkintilloch, where a rising was supposedly taking place.

Numerous arrests followed. Workers suspected of radical sympathies were victimised by employers. Thirty men - mostly weavers - were tried for treason in Glasgow, Dumbarton, Paisley, Ayr, and Stirling. In Stirling, 18 men were sentenced to be hanged, beheaded and quartered. In the end, only three men - Andrew Hardie, John Baird and James Wilson - were actually executed in that barbaric manner.

Long before April 1820, the authorities knew trouble was brewing. They relied on newly constituted police forces, including special constables, to monitor "permissible" gatherings and processions. When serious violence threatened, regular and yeomanry military were summoned. This pattern of response to riot and disorder in Strathclyde was at least partly maintained until 1919.

In 1832, Paisley weavers rioted in the town centre - smashing more than 400 windows - following allegations that doctors deliberately spread cholera to obtain bodies for anatomical research. Troops were called out, the Riot Act was read - and the mob quickly faded away.

By 1848, following the Reform Act of 1832, middle-class town councils were attempting to avoid the overt coercion associated with the ancien regime - exemplified by the "Peterloo Massacre" of 1819, when Manchester yeomanry cavalry charged a radical meeting, killing 11 people and injuring 500. Police forces were part of the new outlook, but remained small, with limited resources. Military intervention persisted - although increasingly as a last resort.

In 1848, Glasgow's small police force had only the "Enrolled Pensioners" - elderly ex-soldiers - as an emergency auxiliary force until special constables could be enrolled. But rapid development of the electric telegraph and railways meant police could now be rapidly reinforced.

Potato blight hit Scotland and Ireland - and the Irish Famine drove thousands of desperate people to seek refuge in Scotland. In spring, 1848, many poor Glaswegians were suffering great hardship. Unemployed labourers were set to breaking stones. Weavers were given webs. Soup tickets and doles of meal were issued.

These measures failed. On March 6, 1848, more than 3000 people gathered on Glasgow Green to hear Chartist orators. Chartists sought widespread reform, including universal suffrage and annual parliaments.

From Glasgow Green, part of the crowd went into the city and gathered outside City Hall, where magistrates were considering relief measures. The police kept a low profile. The crowd dispersed of its own accord.

Most demonstrators remained at Glasgow Green, where they tore up house railings at nearby Monteith Row. Brandishing their new weapons, they headed into the city, looting as they went. Bakeries and provision shops were plundered. Muskets were seized from gunsmiths' premises were ransacked. In Trongate, rioters fired into the air. In Buchanan Street, a fashionable jeweller's shop was broken into. Rioters crossed Jamaica Bridge to loot South Side shops. Bread, oatmeal, cheese and hams were purloined.

The City of Glasgow Police numbered 130 officers and men, armed with batons - against a mob of thousands, many of them armed. The Glasgow Courier remarked:
"The sudden and violent nature of the outbreak seemed for a time to have produced quite a paralysing effect both upon persons in authority and the respectable classes of citizens generally."

Rioters were described as:

"Half-grown lads and mere boys whom but a show of resistance would have been sufficient to quell".

Magistrates called in soldiers from Eglinton Street cavalry barracks. When sabre-wielding troops appeared, rioting ceased. Rioters fled, throwing away their weapons.

Cavalry removed a barricade hastily erected at the head of Saltmarket. It was probably the only barricade erected in the United Kingdom during 1848 - Europe's "Year of

Revolutions".

Placards called on citizens to enrol as special constables. Among those sworn in were hundreds of workers employed by leading engineer Robert Napier. Alexander Smith, an eyewitness, resented special constables:

"Although they did not come into contact with the rioters, the bravery they displayed in cudgeling what unfortunate females, and keelies of tender years, fell into their hands, gave one a lively idea of the prowess they would have exhibited had they met foes worthy of the batons they bore."

Glasgow's police offices were crammed with prisoners. Police recovered about 100 firearms and large quantities of looted food.

Early on March 7, infantry reinforcements arrived by rail. *The Glasgow Courier* waxed prophetic:

"There can be no doubt, now that the first surprise has been overcome, that should any further outbreak occur, the most resolute efforts will be made to quell it in conjunction with the citizens."

On March 7, after a demonstration on Glasgow Green, a mob headed for Bridgeton, where they unsuccessfully appealed for support from silk mill workers. Rioters surged along John Street, Bridgeton, intent on attacking Dalmarnock gasworks and sabotaging the city's supply - a technique employed by revolutionaries in Paris. Police, special constables and enrolled pensioners were pelted with stones. The old soldiers opened fire, killing demonstrator David Carruth. Two other men were fatally wounded.

The volley dispersed the crowd. Rioters carried Carruth's body to Glasgow Cross, where they were halted by infantry with fixed bayonets. The Riot Act was read and the crowd dispersed. That evening, large bodies of special constables patrolled Bridgeton and raided pubs.

On March 8, another meeting was attempted on Glasgow Green. It was broken up by dragoons. By March 11, although troops remained in the city, peace-keeping was carried out by the police, assisted by special constables. Newspapers attacked the police, claiming they had been ill-prepared and unwilling to take decisive action. Chief superintendent Pearce, in command during the riots, resigned.

Once again, the authorities relied on the military. But in two days, 10,000 men had enrolled as special constables. Many rioters were immigrant Catholic Irish - destitute and unskilled. Skilled workers despised the newcomers, while "native" unskilled workers feared immigrants would undercut already low wages.

The Glasgow Courier wrote:

"It was evident that a large proportion of those who seemed most actively bent on mischief belonged to the worst classes of the population, rather than the ranks of the respectable suffering working people. A large number of prisoners are said to be

Irishmen."

A century later, playwright Bertolt Brecht had the beggars in his "Threepenny Opera" chant repeatedly:

"Grub first! Morals later!"

On March 6, 1848, the crowd cried:

"To the shops! Bread! Bread!"

In August 1875, during a celebration by Irish people in Glasgow to mark the centenary of the birth of Irish patriot Daniel O'Connel, which took the form of a procession through Partick, fighting broke out. Many people were injured - and the Riot Act was read.

In the late 19th-century, police accompanied marines to quell land tenure disturbances on islands such as Tiree. In urban Strathclyde, public disorder was mainly linked to localised strikes and lockouts. Soldiers were noticeable by their absence.

Serious large-scale trouble followed the First World War. After four years of high wages, workers were determined to retain and extend their industrial achievements. In 1919, the Clyde Workers Committee, demanded a 40-hour working week.

As tension mounted, troops were sent to Glasgow. Machine guns were mounted on city centre roofs. Tanks were concealed in markets. 1848 seemed back on the agenda. But the military were not used.

On January 31, 1919 - so-called "Black Friday" - police baton-charged thousands of strikers in George Square, Glasgow. Fifteen officers and 50 civilians were injured.

The Herald reported that violence seems to have erupted in the south-east corner of George Square. Young men attempted to halt trams. Whether this was an organised attempt at disruption may never be known. Batons were drawn - and "Black Friday" passed into popular and political history. *The Herald* reported:

"The square soon assumed the appearance of a miniature battlefield. In a melee of that description there can be no respect paid to the individual and all come within the sweep of the weapon of the law."

Demonstrators hurled bottles and stones at police in and around the city centre. At Glasgow Cross, the windows of a tramcar were smashed and its conductor manhandled. In Saltmarket, shop windows were smashed.

Demonstrators from George Square assembled on Glasgow Green, where there were further baton charges. Outside the High Court of Justiciary, nine trams were halted and smashed. Lemonade bottles seized from a passing cart provided ammmunition for protestors. Post-WW1 Scots novelists, such as Lewis Grassic Gibbon in *Grey Granite,* used the image of unemployed men attacking police with bottles to considerable dramatic effect. Through such skilful reworkings, "Black Friday" has attained near-mythic status.

On the evening of January 31, crowds looted stores in Glasgow's Argyle Street. Shop windows were also smashed on the city's South Side. Cigarettes and tobacco were looted. Also on January 31, 1919, Lanarkshire Constabulary confronted striking miners, many of whom were charged with mobbing and rioting. In Blantyre and Bothwell, mobs invaded collieries - where they wrecked offices and attcked police officers. *The Herald* reported:

"With one exception the prisoners are very youthful in appearance, two of them seeming to be mere boys."

In 1922, throwing of bottles and stones followed an anti-unemployment protest in Port Glasgow. Police baton-charged angry crowds. One officer was injured. *The Herald* reported:

"Men were seen carrying off hams, whole cheeses, bottles of sweets, and a great variety of articles."

During the General Strike of 1926, police and strikers clashed in Glasgow, Lanarkshire, Greenock, Port Glasgow, Clydebank, and Ayrshire. Strikers tried to halt transport services run by students and other volunteers. While there were numerous injuries, use of potentially lethal weapons does not feature in contemporary or later accounts.

There was isolated sabotage of railway lines, involving use of mining explosives - again dramatised by Lewis Grassic Gibbon in *Cloud Howe*. Significantly, Gibbon's fictional railway saboteurs belonged to a community's "angry young men". In Lanarkshire, police were pelted with stones while protecting railway repair squads.

In his history of the City of Glasgow Police, *The Thin Blue Line* (1973), former police officer Douglas Grant suggests that public estimation of police actually increased in the wake of 1926. The military were largely used for "show".

In 1932, soaring unemployment and benefits cuts led to confrontations between police and rioters in many parts of Strathclyde. In Kilbirnie, Ayrshire, hundreds of unemployed people mobbed a meeting of the parish council, demanding that councillors resisted the hated means test. Demonstrators sang "Banks and Braes" and "Rowan Tree" - before breaking into "The Red Flag". Protestors attempted to storm the council meeting. Police drew batons and dispersed the crowd. The incident has passed into North Ayrshire folklore.

Also in 1932, police in Paisley baton-charged demonstrators alleged to be about to storm the town's sheriff court building, where men were on trial on charges of mobbing and rioting after an earlier protest against the means test. There were similar incidents in Greenock and Port Glasgow.

Growing prosperity from 1930s' rearmament programmes probably reduced tensions in Strathclyde. Serious rioting in the UK did not resurface until the 1970s and 1980s, with the focus shifting to grievances among young people from ethnic minority backgrounds in London and the Midlands of England.

Strathclyde, with a small ethnic population, dispersed and largely self-employed, avoided such disturbances. There were small-scale "copy-cat" incidents involving young people in deprived housing schemes. In Drumchapel, Glasgow, police vehicles were firebombed. Although major confrontations between police and rioters have been largely absent from Strathclyde since the 1930s, trouble can still erupt. After Rangers FC lost to Celtic FC in the Scottish Cup Final of 1980, at Hampden Park, Glasgow, fans invaded the pitch. Mounted police charged to break up the fighting. There were 210 arrests. One hundred people were injured, including four police officers. *The Herald* reported:

"In the middle a handful of policemen fought to keep separate battling fans. The mounted police drew their long riot batons for the first time in Glasgow since the General Strike of 1926. Only when they charged did the warring fans retreat."

The Herald also reported drunken fans attacking staff at a Glasgow hospital:

"In the midst of the mayhem, it was impressive to watch the way in which the police, many ignoring their injuries, managed to calm and control the situation. For some, their uniforms drenched in spittle from the fans, it would be hours before they were officially off duty. For a time, it was mob rule, with hordes of fans, most of them drunken teenagers, jostling, swaggering, jeering, swearing, and singing along main routes in the city centre."

"Black Fridays" are always a possibility. The constable of 1847 would have understood that. ☐

SHEBEENS AND STEAMING

FROM the outset of policing in Strathclyde, alcohol in all its aspects was a major preoccupation for law enforcement. Strathclyde Police Museum displays containers used in the past to smuggle stolen alcohol - usually from Clydeside docks areas. The drunks' barrow, last used in the 1920s, is another reminder of how officers had to deal nightly with the consequences of alcohol abuse.

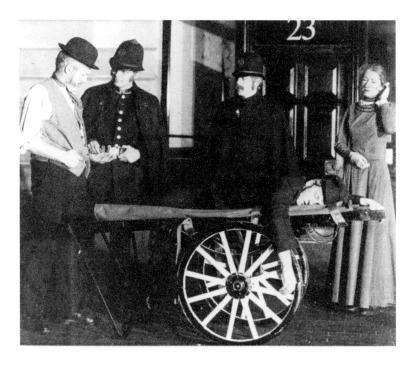

Illicit distilling in Scotland is normally associated with romantically portrayed smugglers and moonshiners in the Highlands and Islands. In fact, such products only reached comparatively wealthy people in urban Scotland.

Large quantities of less wholesome *uisge beatha* were distilled in West of Scotland towns - with Glasgow a noted centre for the covert industry. In 1815, *The Herald* reported:

"On Monday night, Mr Anderson, Supervisor of Excise, and two of his officers, discovered an illicit still of nearly 50 gallons between Union Place and Mitchell Street, Glasgow. Two men were working it, whom they detained, while they proceeded to destroy utensils and raw materials. The still was charged with low wines at the time, which the officers allowed to flow into the street. One of the smugglers set fire to the spirit, and escaped in the confusion.

"The fire was extinguished, and officers demolished tuns and had gone some distance with the worm etc, when the fellows who had previously escaped returned with about 12 of their gang and soon recovered possession of their utensils. The officer who was knocked down was severely cut on the head. This is only one instance of the atrocious audacity of the smugglers. It has been calculated that from three to five hundred illicit stills are at work in this city and vicinity."

One 19th-century shebeener described a supplier of stolen whisky, who deployed concealed containers similar to the items displayed in the museum. When the whisky thief entered the shebeen, he appeared to be about 18 stones in weight. After divesting himself of his load, he appeared to have lost eight stones.

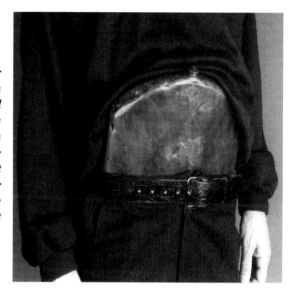

In 1840s' Glasgow, drunkenness was the single largest category of arrests. In 1850, there were 2000 licensed premises in the city - one for every 160 persons - along with an unknown tally of unlicensed shebeens.

One shebeener's "apprenticeship" consisted of learning to mix concoctions which sound very much like "rocket fuel" or "electric soup". One shebeen staple consisted of one gallon of raw grain whisky mixed with five gallons of water, to which were added sixpence-worth of methylated spirits and "a pint of raspberry vinegar to colour".

Other shebeeners' beverages included a mix of two gallons of whisky, three gallons of water, and sixpence-worth of meths. One mid-19th century shebeen in Glasgow's Saltmarket was said to have been so busy it employed 15 waiters. It was claimed that the establishment made £80 a week. It also passed itself off as a social club. Chief constables were still complaining about this practice as late as the 1950s.

Every year between 1860 and 1870, between 45,000 and 64,000 drunks were apprehended by City of Glasgow police. Helplessly drunk citizens were conveyed to police stations in drunks' barrows.

Victorian beer was powerful stuff. Ales with an original gravity of 1060 were common. Long-matured "old ales" were even stronger. But most drunks probably owed their condition to raw, fiery whisky - illicit or legal. Until 1915, there was no law compelling whisky distillers to mature their product for a minimum period prior to sale. Victorian whisky has been described as "a torchlight procession down the throat". It frequently drove imbibers berserk.

Perils of shebeen whisky were even greater. Much of it wasn't whisky anyway. It was based on methylated spirits - known as "finish". Shebeens received a boost from the operations of the Forbes Mackenzie Act of 1853, which closed pubs on Sundays. In 1859, Glasgow police seized a still from Thomas Scott, proprietor of the Working Men's Refreshment Rooms, Gallowgate. In that year alone, 603 Glaswegians were prosecuted for shebeening.

Only "bona fide travellers" were allowed to drink on Sundays. Drouthy Glaswegians and their Paisley counterparts passed each other on the road between the two towns. On Clyde steamers, Sunday drinking remained legal until 1882. "Booze cruises" caused problems for police. In 1877, **The Herald** reported:

"On arrival at Greenock, the police were called to take into custody several peace-breakers. Their friends set up a stout resistance and the police had to satisfy themselves with apprehending two of the ringleaders."

Drunken outings on Clyde steamers gave rise to the term "steaming".

Shebeening was still widespread in the late-19th century. "Mother McGuire" kept a notorious shebeen in Glasgow's Saltmarket. She was also a resetter - a "fence". As with United States "speakeasys" during the mid-20th century, passwords were necessary to gain admittance to Mother McGuire's "hostelry".

Mother McGuire had ingenious methods of avoiding detection and arrest:

"There is a hoist of box form running between the upper and lower flats. A rope hidden in the wall is pulled, and the liquor is taken to the upper flat. Should officers enter both flats, the rope is pulled until the hoist reaches half-way."

Mother McGuire's 'finish' was said to have lethal consequences, too.

"She procured it for about 2d per gill, and retailed it at 6d and 1/- per glass. Men and women have been found dead in shebeens from overdoses of it. A single firm in Leith, during the short space of two months, disposed of 3000 gallons of methylated spirits."

Glasgow's first great international exhibition, in Kelvingrove Park, closed on November 11, 1888, amid boisterous scenes. Hordes of young men, mostly students, invaded the exhibition's Bachelors' Cafe, getting seriously drunk and smashing glasses. Since then recently introduced German lager was on sale, the incident could have been Glasgow's first encounter with "lager louts". Considerable latitude was given to Victorian students, most of whom belonged to well-off families.

In the early 1890s, as a consequence of Civic Improvement Acts, Glasgow Corporation actually owned about 30 pubs. The corporation was heavily pro-temperance - and as old buildings were replaced with model tenements, pubs were outlawed. Anti-pub municipal philosophy endured into the post-WW2 era, leaving giant Glasgow housing schemes such as Easterhouse and Drumchapel without pubs. Residents travelled into the city centre at weekends. With pubs shutting at 10pm, mostly male drinkers "swilled" between 9pm and closing time. It was common for buses full of angry drunks to be driven straight to Glasgow police stations. Bus crews were at frequent risk of assault.

Between 1853 and 1910, police forces had to cope with the consequences of decisions made by influential pro-temperance MPs and councillors. In July 1905, Greenock's hard-line magistrates shut the town's pubs on Fair Monday. Hundreds of people crowded onto trams bound for Gourock - where pubs were open. *The Herald* reported:

"On reaching Gourock, crowds congregated around public houses, which did a roaring trade. Men and women in various stages of intoxication staggered about the streets. Early in the afternoon, the police cells were full, and the police wisely decided to allow the drunks to sleep off their debauch where they had fallen. Many drunks were also sprawled along the seafront at Ashton. There was considerable fighting, and women also took part in disgraceful brawls."

Ten o'clock closing was imposed on Glasgow in 1904 - with the predictable result that beer and whisky were consumed proportionately faster between the hours of nine and ten. In 1903, there had been 14,176 prosecutions for drunkenness in Glasgow, and 9298 convictions. By 1906, the drunks' barrows were in considerable demand, as prosecutions rose to 20,247 and convictions increased to 13,239.

Shebeeners and illicit distillers still flourished on the eve of WW1. Their activities, already threatening public health, also caused public disorder. When police raided a shebeen in Cowcaddens, Glasgow, in 1913, the proprietor ditched the evidence in spectacular fashion. *The Herald* reported:

"Baskets laden with bottles of beer and whisky were heaved promiscuously into the street. At both front and back windows, the expedient was adopted, and the pavements and the back court were littered with broken bottles and spilt liquor."

Under the Defence of the Realm Act, pub hours were curtailed. "Munitions Ale" was much weaker than pre-war beers. The price of whisky soared. Between 1914 and 1920, duty on whisky rose from 14/9d per proof gallon to 72/6d per gallon.

For policing, restrictions brought renewed problems. Shebeeners again filled the gap. In 1916, Govan shebeener Sarah Gillon was fined £30 for selling a half bottle of homemade whisky. She was arrested again in 1917 - for selling whisky described as "undrinkable".

Wages were rising fast - and there was little legal alcohol for citizens to purchase. Theft and shebeening remained very serious problems for short-staffed police forces burdened with wartime responsibilities. Legitimate publicans resented restrictions, shebeeners were blatant and occasionally violent - and temperance campaigners were still active. All made demands on the police.

After WW1, drink prices remained high - giving rise to the lament "Twelve an a Tanner a Bottle", made famous by Scots comedian Will Fyfe. To some extent, new leisure facilities such as super cinemas and skating rinks reduced the popularity of pubs during the interwar years. But illegal activities associated with alcohol were still common In 1920, police arrested an illicit distiller in Shettleston, who claimed that his bubbling, smoking equipment was "an Irish musical instrument".

In 1926, police and excise officers seized an illicit still in rural Ayrshire. The still was owned by a Glasgow newsagent, who might have been purveying its output in his shop.

In 1927, a Glasgow tinsmith accused of illicit distilling admitted using his trade skills to make stills for his friends and neighbours. Such activities were accompanied by widespread thefts of legitimate whisky - which was sold to both licensees and shebeeners.

But in the 1930s, mass unemployment and high prices meant that shebeeners still flourished. Consumption of cheap "alternatives" such as methylated spirits rose. It was claimed many Glaswegians consumed huge quantities of an "obnoxious drink" composed of meths boiled with wine and vegetables and then fermented. In 1934, Edward Hilley, arrested for fiddling his gas meter in Bridgeton, Glasgow, told a court:

"I needed the gas for the still which was for making whisky."

During 1935, Glasgow officers arrested 495 men and 95 women for meths drinking. There had been only 277 and 77 respectively in 1931. Shebeeners became more sophisticated at passing themselves off as legitimate social clubs - a stratagem which had begun in the 1860s. In 1936, Glasgow chief constable Percy Sillitoe called such establishments "legalised drinking dens" and warned councillors that they were increasingly difficult to supervise. In that year, legal restrictions on sales of meths were widely welcomed by Strathclyde's police forces. But seven shebeeners were still convicted in Glasgow. In 1937, newspapers warned of alleged widespread consumption of "boot polish cocktail" - lemonade mixed with meths, metal polish and boot polish. In 1938 - despite growing prosperity created by rearmament programmes - 26 shebeeners were convicted in Glasgow.

By 1939, only one woman was convicted of drinking meths in the city - along with 39 men. But 15 shebeeners were up in court.

During WW2, huge influxes of war workers and service personnel poured into Strathclyde. Shebeeners took full advantage. In 1943, the head of Glasgow's American Red Cross Club complained bitterly about the effects of raw shebeen whisky on US service personnel.

Thieving of alcohol became a virtual epidemic during WW2 - encouraged by blackout and the limitations of wartime policing. Whisky vanished in huge quantities from rail depots, docks, warehouses and pubs. Incidents redolent of "Whisky Galore" weren't limited to isolated Hebridean islands. On November 29, 1940, *The Herald* reported:

"A most audacious theft was carried out of a large quantity of whisky which was to be exported from Glasgow to America. The whisky was put on a lorry, which was driven away in the wrong direction and the whisky stolen."

During 1940, 142 perfume drinkers were arrested in Glasgow, along with eight drinkers of surgical spirit and 23 meths drinkers.

As the price of a bottle of legitimate whisky rose to 17/6d, illicit distilling helped make up shortfalls. The mining district of Shettleston became known as "Glasgow's distilling centre" - possibly because miners could readily obtain coal to fire stills. Govan was reputed to be the main focus for shebeening.

It seems that when legal alcohol is restricted - for whatever reasons - some people will try anything to obtain drink. During war work in Inverclyde shipyards, Scots poet Hugh MacDiarmid claimed to have seen men drink industrial spirits from ships' compasses.

"Respectable" publicans let it be known they were in the market for supplies from any source and at any price. Occasionally, such biters were bit. In 1944, a Glasgow man defrauded a pub manageress of £288 by pretending he could obtain 288 bottles of whisky at £1 a bottle. The whisky was never delivered.

In the post-war years of economic austerity, shebeening continued - along with thefts of whisky and instances of illicit distilling. But returning prosperity brought new problems and challenges for policing and society. Following WW1, communities could hold "veto polls" which led to effective prohibition in many parts of Strathclyde. Best known such instance was the town of Kirkintilloch which remained "dry" until veto polls were abolished in 1976.

But by the early 1960s, the temperance movement had lost virtually all influence in Scotland. On April 14, 1962, *The Herald* reported:

"Stewarton, Ayrshire, a 'dry' town for more than 40 years, was yesterday granted six liquor licences - one hotel, two public houses, and three off sales. Recently, the town held a poll and decided to end the 'dry' spell which started in 1920."

Shebeening, linked with theft and illicit distilling, remained a serious problem. Sunday opening was still banned, and pubs shut at 10pm. Public attitudes could be ambiguous. The media portrayed some shebeeners as "Robin Hood" figures.

For neighbours of Iolande Gherardi, 645 Argyle Street, Glasgow, there was nothing remotely romantic about shebeening. During the 1960s, Ms Gherardi appeared constantly in court, charged with "trafficking in liquor without possessing a licence".

On occasion, her flat was found to contain up to 26 gallons of alcohol. Complainers alleged taxis arrived at all hours. In 1962 alone, Ms Gherardi was fined a total of £1000 for shebeening. The problem only ended when police discovered that Ms Gherardi was an Italian citizen and she was deported.

The Licensing (Scotland) Act 1976 was widely welcomed as a means of eliminating frantic drinking between 9pm and 10pm. The Act abolished veto polls, legitimised Sunday drinking, and gave police additional powers over licensed clubs.

Nonetheless, police and addiction campaigners continued to express concern about alcohol consumption in Strathclyde. As pubs opened later, particularly in town centres, they attracted younger people - and complaints about excessive noise and encouragement of under-age drinking. Pub and club operators announced their intention to remain open until 2am whenever and wherever possible. On September 22, 1976, *The Herald* reported:

"Alcoholism in Scotland is heading towards epidemic proportions and may affect the lives of 1,250,000 Scots by the mid-1980s, according to the annual report of the Scottish Council on Alcoholism."

The organisation called for comprehensive alcohol services, including community-based detoxification and rehabilitation services in major population areas, along with education at school level upwards.

In December 1976, Strathclyde Regional Council claimed that the West of Scotland's "frightening legacy of barbarian drinking habits" cost ratepayers at least œ20m a year.

The link between alcohol and offending remained. *The Herald* reported:

"Dr A Balfour Sclare, consultant pyschiatrist at Duke Street hospital, Glasgow, disclosed that 70% of persons charged with murder in Scotland had drink problems, and between 75% and 90% of prisoners had drink problems."

Patterns of drinking began to alter rapidly with movements of population and changing social habits. In the 19th century - and for much of the 20th century - working people (mostly men) drank in pubs, while middle class citizens drank at home and obtained their supplies from licensed grocers. The late-20th century brought the rise of "classless" off-licences - including national chains such as Victoria Wine, Thresher and Oddbins. UK national supermarket chains perform similar functions. In Scotland as a whole, between 1980 and 1996, the number of pubs increased from 4472 to 5070. But off-sales licences rose from 4899 to 6365.

Entertainment licenses in Scotland between 1980 and 1996 rose from 169 to 850 - mainly because of the spread of clubs and discotheques in cities and large towns. But from time to time, there were complaints from press, public and politicians that discos were noisy, socially disruptive, and inclined to cause young people to drink too much. Such complaints have been heard before. The 19th-century temperance movement made almost precisely such claims regarding music halls, mainly in Glasgow.

So, are criticisms of discos and clubs based on genuine observation and evidence - or are they 'moral panics'? In dealing with drink, as with other legal and social issues, policing has to deal also with such fairly obvious 'competing perspectives'.

Distinctions between various sorts of licensed premises in the late-20th century could be blurring rapidly. Between 1980 and 1996, restaurant licenses in Scotland increased from 921 to 1488. But in the same period, many pubs also began to sell food. And pubs are also recognisably places of entertainment.

Long-standing prohibitions on music in pubs in Glasgow, for example - supposedly introduced because of official fears that "Republican" or "Orange" songs might lead to breaches of the peace, assaults or rioting - are fading into folk memory. Pubs feature live bands, disco nights, quizzes and talent contests. Music and food now seem almost synonymous with consumption of alcohol in the West of Scotland.

By and large, such changes have been hailed as evidence of social progress - with the implication that modern policing is not overly concerned with alcohol-related issues. But in the 1990s, increasing public concern focussed on outdoors drinking, often by young people consuming cheap fortified wines such as Buckfast. Increasingly, local authorities throughout the West of Scotland introduced by-laws outlawing consumption of drink in outdoor locations. Such restrictions were imposed on events such as Dunoon's Cowal Games, leading to complaints that the character of such institutions in the "folk calendar" had been irretrievably damaged. Other opinion hailed "cleaning up of the streets".

Prohibition of outdoors drinking also became linked with so-called "curfews" imposed by police on young people in urban areas - and revealed clear differences between sections of press and public opinion. Some newspapers welcomed "curfews" and quoted parents as glad to know that their children were supervised by police officers. Other sections of the press labelled such developments as oppressive and doomed to failure and quoted members of the public who claimed their children were being "picked on and pushed about".

The long and ever-changing history of the relationship between policing and alcohol in the West of Scotland reflects the role of policing in general. Policing must operate with public consent - and it has never been entirely clear who or what accurately represents that public consent. And one citizen's moderate drinking is another citizen's definition of alcohol abuse. It has ever been thus.□

SHADOW OF A GUNMAN

A NUMBER of firearms used in offences since the 19th century are displayed in Strathclyde Police Museum - including weapons used to kill or injure police officers.

During the 19th century, firearms were frequently used for criminal purposes in Strathclyde. In 1820, the County Patrol - a rudimentary police force operating in Bridgeton, then a village on the edge of Glasgow - interrupted a gang burgling a shop. One of the thieves fired a horse pistol, wounding a patrol member. Most of the gang were arrested, including "notorious character" John Sharp - who'd fired the shot.

Firearms were used during industrial disputes and radical uprisings. Also in 1820, "an armed band of ruffians" fired shots into a house in Dale Street, Bridgeton, occupied by workers from John Barr & Co's Greenhead Mill.

In 1839, footpads held up a gentleman in Glasgow - and at pistol point robbed him of 7/-. One of the robbers apologised, explaining he'd been driven to crime "by want of employment".

In 1870, Parliament passed a Gun Licences Act - but this was essentially a tax measure, ensuring that citizens purchased at post offices a licence costing 10/-. The Act lasted until 1967. Late-19th century attempts at serious firearms legislation were "talked out" of the House of Commons by MPs who claimed possession of firearms was a fundamental component of "civil rights".

At the turn of the century, firearms were readily available in most parts of Strathclyde. Widespread participation in the Volunteer movement - a forerunner of the Territorial Army - meant many young men knew how to use firearms.

Ironmongers more or less freely sold revolvers, shotguns and rifles - and advertised openly in newspapers and magazines. The Pistols Act of 1903 simply required that retailers registered purchasers, who had to produce their 10/- licences at the point of sale.

Large numbers of Volunteers served in the Boer War alongside regular troops - and it is possible that numbers of these men brought firearms back to Scotland. Lethal weapons were also extremely common in rural Strathclyde.

There were frequent deliberate or accidental shootings. On June 6, 1909, *The Herald* reported:

"A man named Joseph Wilson, residing at Moss Street, Paisley, was admitted to the Royal Infirmary, Glasgow, last night, suffering from serious injuries sustained in a shooting accident which occurred in the Glasgow Rifle Club, Howard Street.
"Wilson, an expert shot, has won a number of medals in shooting competitions, and is said to have been engaged in a contest with a friend for a wager. He had a clay pipe in his mouth, and his opponent was trying to shoot it out."

Incidents such as London's notorious "Siege of Sydney Street" in 1911, in which bank

18

robbers held off a large force of police and soldiers, sparked considerable debate about firearms and crime. Glasgow's chief constable argued that if officers were to be armed on occasions of danger, training would be of the essence:

"A revolver in untrained hands is a dangerous weapon."

There's no evidence that Sherlock Holmes and Dr Watson had any training in use of hand guns - despite Watson's Army background. Right up to the great fictional detective's "Last Bow" in 1914, he carried and used revolvers without hindrance from the law, other than his 10/- licence.

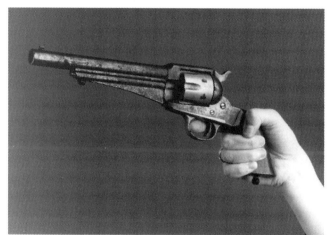

This weapon was taken from a real US cowboy, found waving it about in 1890s' Glasgow. As far as is known , no one was hurt- but accidental shootings are just as deadly as deliberate use of firearms.

In 1914, 30 rifle-carrying Orangemen marched through Glasgow, escorting the colours of the "Ulster Volunteers" - loyalist militants pledged to support Unionists and Protestants in Northern Ireland. As the law stood, such public displays of privately held firearms were perfectly legal.

During WW1, many shootings were consequences of horse-play or accidents. In 1916, a soldier on leave was travelling with his rifle in a tramcar in Sauchiehall Street. The weapon was accidentally discharged, and the round struck and killed another soldier in the street.

Firearms were used to settle arguments. On June 7, 1915, *The Herald* reported:

"A remarkable shooting affair occurred on Saturday at the North British Diesel Engine Works, South Street, Whiteinch, Glasgow. A dispute about payment of wages took place between Mr John Holloway, works manager, and a foreman who was due to leave the firm. It is alleged that while talking to Mr Holloway, the foreman drew a five-chambered revolver from his pocket, and shot him in the left hip."

Elizabeth Campbell (13) was fatally wounded in a rifle range accident at a Glasgow fairground. In 1916, six members of Glasgow's Cowboys gang were each fined 10/6d for entering a city pub and threatening customers with a toy gun.

After WW1, tens of thousands of firearms were brought home by discharged soldiers - mostly as keepsakes or for "shooting for the pot". It was always rather unlikely that items such as Lewis guns (light machine guns extensively during WW1 and in the early stages of WW2) - which turned up in raids and amnesties during the 1920s - would be used in murders or bank robberies.

As late as the 1950s, after firearms law had been tightened, elderly farmers were still appearing in court, charged with possessing .303 Lee Enfield rifles taken home from the 1914-18 conflict. Some seemed to have difficulty understanding that they had committed serious offences.

Late on the evening of January 18, 1919. Glasgow PC James Campbell went to investigate noises in a back court near the city's Parkhead Cross. He was confronted by a man whom he challenged and attempted to detain. During a scuffle, two shots were fired. PC Campbell was hit in the neck and abdomen. The man bolted. PC Campbell died in hospital on January 20, 1919. Despite massive police inquiries, PC Campbell's killer was never identified. Witnesses described a young man who boarded a tram in the area, shortly after the shooting, and who seemed to be in a breathless and excited state. But all leads led nowhere.

The Parkhead shooting shocked police, press, politicians and the public. First serious firearms legislation appeared in 1920 - but even at that there were dispensations for "war trophies".

On May 4, 1921, a van carrying an Irish Republican activist from court to Duke Street prison, Glasgow, was ambushed in the city's Drygate, by at least 30 armed men - who attempted to release the prisoner. One of the escorting police officers, Inspector Robert Johnston, was killed instantly.

The Herald reported:

"Happening in broad daylight in the heart of the city, the murder, associated as it was with a fierce revolver fight between police and desperadoes, created a tremendous sensation throughout the West of Scotland as the facts became known. Bullets rattled against the prison wall, leaving marks in the masonry."

Growth of popular low-priced cars combined with large numbers of unemployed men who had learned to drive during WW1 to create "motor bandits" - who in the late 1920s and early 1930s contributed to a moral panic in the press. "Smash and grab" motor bandits robbed banks, jewellers shops, and other "high value" targets. Similar panic gripped the United States. with the public exhibiting a "split" attitude to such criminals. On both sides of the Herring Pond, the public simultaneously regarded motor bandits as folk heroes *and* dangerous desperadoes.

In 1934, *The Herald* reported:

"The need for rapid communication and greater police mobility to combat the motor

bandit is urged in the annual report of HM Inspector of Constabulary in Scotland. The inspector also recommends the installation of wireless apparatus in patrol cars."

In 1928, a Territorial Army soldier in a moving train on the outskirts of Glasgow fired his rifle at a crow. The round killed a young woman walking with her fiance on Cathkin Braes - two miles away. The soldier was jailed for three months.

In 1935, a Glasgow firearms amnesty yielded 190 pistols, 35 rifles, 2500 rounds of ammunition - and a collection of shells and grenades, some of them live. The Firearms (Scotland) (Amendment) Rules 1935 restricted amounts of ammunition which could be held by licensed gun owners. By 1937, "war trophies" dispensations were phased out.

In 1939, an unemployed Glasgow man threatened a shop assistant with a revolver - and escaped with sixpence. Newspapers made fun of the incident - but a young woman could have been killed or wounded for a ludicrous sum of money. The robber probably had no intention of using his weapon. But the consequences of accident are as horrific as deliberate intent.

During WW2, service weapons again found their way into Civvy Street. In 1943, five Glasgow boys took part in "bombing escapades" after stealing grenades from a Home Guard munitions dump.

Hold-ups involved hand guns and sawn-off shotguns. Post offices were particular targets during WW2. Wartime lighting restrictions and depleted police forces encouraged such activities.

On October 26, 1943, *The Herald* reported:

"Bullets were fired through windows of two Glasgow tramcars, sending glass splinters among startled passengers, in two mysterious shooting incidents about 8.30 last night in Sauchiehall Street, Glasgow.

"In one case the sound of a shot rang out near Charing Cross, and a bullet, apparently fired from the street, penetrated an upper-deck window of a Mosspark-bound tramcar. Glass splinters sprayed over a passenger, but he was not injured. A tramcar on the Clarkston route was the 'target' of a second shot further west in Sauchiehall Street, a bullet leaving a hole in a lower-deck window. Again no one was injured."

In 1944, railway workers in Partick, Glasgow, came under fire from a sub-machine gun - possibly stolen from Home Guard stocks - and fired by two young men. Police estimated up to 100 rounds were fired in the direction of the workers. No one was arrested for the offence.

In 1952, Glasgow PC John McLeod was shot dead while attempting to arrest a 17-year-old youth in the city's Hyndland district. Another officer was seriously wounded. The 17-year-old shot himself.

In 1956, amid lurid publicity, Lanarkshire officers arrested murderer Peter Manuel - who had shot six people in the area. Manuel had thrown his guns into the Clyde near the suspension bridge linking Clyde Street with South Portland Street, Glasgow. Police first used a giant electro-magnet to search for Manuel's murder weapons, which were eventually recovered by a diver.

In 1961, a guns amnesty in Glasgow brought in 561 firearms, along with 13,993 rounds of ammunition. In 1965, members of the public surrendered 41 rifles, 208 revolvers, and 12,477 rounds of ammunition - along with 254 shells and grenades.

In 1969, James Griffiths, suspected of assault and robbery in Ayr, began firing when police went to his flat in Glasgow's Holyrood Crescent. Six civilians were injured. Griffiths then drove through North- west Glasgow, firing indiscriminately at passers-by. After shooting a car driver, he burst into a pub in Possil Road, where he threatened staff and customers before fatally wounding pensioner William Hughes. After stealing a lorry, he wounded two more civilians before heading for Springburn. Police guided playing children to safety as Griffiths began firing from a flat in Kay Street, Springburn. He injured two civilians, including an 8-year-old boy.

Two armed officers, Chief Superintendent Malcolm Finlayson and Detective Sergeant Ian Smith, approached the door of the flat. Chief Superintendent Finlayson fired through the letter box, killing Griffiths. He had aimed at the gunman's shoulder, but the bullet ricocheted and pierced his aorta. Weeks later, the chief superintendent said:

"I killed a man: that's something I will not readily forget."

On 30 December, 1969, three Glasgow police officers were shot by an ex-police constable who had taken part in an armed robbery at a bank in Renfrewshire. The officers had seen the ex-constable and his associates carrying a box and a suitcase into a flat in Allison Street, Glasgow, shortly after the robbery.

As the police searched the flat, the ex-constable shot Inspector Andrew Hyslop, Constable Edward Barnett, and acting Detective Constable Angus Mckenzie. Detective Constable McKenzie died almost immediately. Constable Barnett was mortally wounded. Inspector Hyslop survived, but as a result of his experience and wounds left the City of Glasgow Police in 1971. Parts of the bullet which struck him remained deeply embedded in his neck.

But police in Strathclyde remained firmly opposed to routine carrying of firearms. In 1978, **The Herald** pointed out that arming of police officers could prove futile. Routine arming of police would not necessarily reduce firearms offences.

"The most recent occasion when a number of police were given guns was during the trial of Walter Norval at the High Court in Glasgow after attempts had been made to burn down the court building. Armed police escorted the accused persons from Barlinnie prison to the court. Armed police surrounded the court and were placed inside until the trial ended. On that occasion police only suspected that armed men would attempt to free the accused."

Most shootings are unexpected - and, in UK national terms, Strathclyde is not a particularly violent area in respect of firearms-related offences. In the late-1980s, it was estimated that 75% of firearms-related crime in the UK took place in the Metropolitan Police area.

In 1981, a series of armed robberies in Strathclyde echoed the era of "motor bandits". A gang armed with sawn-off shotguns stole £50,000 from a Lanarkshire car auction firm. The raid followed two similar incidents in Glasgow. Police suspected they were the work of the same gang. The firm's MD told *The Herald:*

"We were only a few yards from the office when a Cortina rammed my car on the side, forcing me off the road. Two men wearing grotesque old men masks smashed the car windows. They pointed shotguns at us and said: 'If you don't hand over the money, we'll blow your heads off.' They escaped in another Cortina. It was a terrifying experience."

In the early 1980s, Strathclyde Police had to deal with a number of instances in which supporters of terrorist groups in Northern Ireland obtained firearms in Scotland. In 1981, *The Herald* reported:

"A man claiming to be a spokesman for the Ulster Defence Association in Glasgow told viewers of Ulster Television last night that arms and explosives were regularly smuggled into the province, but weapons had recently been held back for use, if necessary, in Scotland.
"The man, shown in silhouette, was filmed in Glasgow last week. He claimed a shipment of seven rifles, 10 sub-machine guns, and 10lb of explosive had been transported to Ulster last Thursday."

In 1983, *The Herald* reported:

"Armed raiders who burst into a sub-post office in the centre of Glasgow yesterday fired a shotgun at a door during the raid, the 23rd in which weapons have been carried in Strathclyde in eight weeks. The raid has led to renewed demands for severe restraint on access to shotguns."

The paper added that many shotguns found their way to criminals, after being stolen from private households.

In the 1980s, many workers in Strathclyde were still paid weekly in cash - giving robbers ample opportunities. In 1984, *The Herald* reported:

"Armed raiders escaped with more than £40,000 in a wages snatch at Clyde Dock Engineering, Govan, Glasgow. The robbery took place in the afternoon as 46 of the firm's 220 workers were about to be paid off."

In October 1984, three boys aged 14, 15, and 16, were sentenced to detention after firing rifles and shotguns wildly during a 16-hour siege following a break-in at a sports shop. *The Herald* reported:

"The police siege followed a break-in at Pitchers sports shop in Moss Street, Paisley, last June. Ambulances and fire services were called in, the lives of the public were put in danger, and train services had to be diverted during the fusillade of shots."

In the 1990s, armed robberies at banks declined rapidly, as a result of of security technology such as time-delayed safes and CCTV cameras. Cash containers carried in security vehicles which automatically cover banknotes with indelible dye if removed from vehicles - reduced attacks on security vans. Payment of workers in cash is now rare - as are "wages bags".

But firearms continue to be used in armed robberies at off-licenses, post offices and small shops. Often, such offences are carried out with replica firearms. Frequently, these robberies are carried by people seeking cash with which to purchase drugs. For staff in such premises, replica firearms are as frightening as real weapons. Replica firearms are intentionally realistic.

Police, politicians and sections of the press have sought legal bans on replica firearms. The murder of 13 children and a teacher at Dunblane Primary School, on March 13, 1996, led to vociferous public demands for intensified legal control of firearms. Parliament outlawed large-calibre handguns in 1997, and small-calibre handguns in 1998.

Shotguns were not covered by such legislation, and are still used in offences in Strathclyde. Between 1994 and 1998, 29 murders were carried out using firearms in Strathclyde. Of these, 20 were carried out with handguns. In virtually none of these cases were the handguns legally held by perpetrators.

Thomas Hamilton, the killer of the Dunblane children and teacher, legally held his collection of handguns. Some police officers argue take the view that while the banning of handguns formerly legally held for sporting purposes is socially desirable, such measures are unlikely to affect "underworld" weapons.

South of the border, drugs-related criminals - such as Afro-Caribbean "Yardie" gangs - are alleged to deploy weapons such as AK-47 assault rifles and sub-machine-guns. This problem has not affected the West of Scotland to any degree.

Murders involving firearms in Strathclyde continue - most probably linked to "turf wars" among drugs traders.

In 1900, firearms could be obtained "over the counter" - few questions asked. By 1998, unauthorised possession of guns meant draconian penalties for offenders.

"Yardie" gangs, given their ethnic origin, would find it hard to operate within Strathclyde with its small ethnic minority population. The "Russian Mafia" might be a different matter.

Firearms imported illegally from regions such as Eastern Europe could feature in drugs-related offending.

In the light of such possibilities, Strathclyde's thin blue line will remain vigilant on the matter of firearms.

Demands for restrictions on firearms have invariably followed distressing incidents such as the Dunblane killings and various shootings of police officers. The stable door has often only been closed after some *very* bloody horses have bolted. ☐

POISON AND PIETY

STRATHCLYDE Police Museum features some of Victorian Scotland's best-known murderers and murders. The 1857 case of Madeleine Smith - a "spoilt little rich girl" accused of poisoning her socially inferior lover - has been reworked constantly by film and TV producers. The trial, sentence and subsequent pardon of Oscar Slater has become one of Scotland's most infamous miscarriages of justice - and involved Sir Arthur Conan Doyle, creator of Sherlock Holmes and Dr Watson.

MADELEINE SMITH

THE verdict of "not proven" is unique to Scotland. Cynics define it as meaning "We know you did it, but we just can't prove it." So it was in the High Court at Edinburgh on 9 July, 1857, at the conclusion of the trial for murder of 21-year-old Madeleine Smith - daughter of a wealthy Glasgow architect. She was indicted for having poisoned her lover, 33-year-old impecunious clerk Pierre Emile L'Angelier, a native of Jersey.

Madeleine Smith

Did she murder L'Angelier and is the verdict of "not proven" a safeguard for innocent people?

Pierre Emile L'Angelier

A simple, love-lorn poor man or a fortune hunting Lothario? The verdict is still open.

25

The trial became perhaps Scotland's greatest legal *cause celebre* - with Madeleine's steamy love letters read out in court.

She first met L'Angelier in April 1855. By June 1856, they were lovers. Madeleine's father - owner of a substantial town house in Glasgow's fashionable Blythswood Square - would not have countenanced L'Angelier as a son in law. In January 1857, Madeleine became engaged to William Minnoch, a prosperous middle-aged Glasgow merchant. In letters, she called L'Angelier her "beloved husband" and described herself as his "devoted wife".

Besotted with Madeleine, L'Angelier refused to end their passionate affair. He threatened to show her letters to her father.

L'Angelier came at night to a ground-floor window of her family home in Blythswood Square, where Madeleine plied him with cups of cocoa. During February and March 1857, L'Angelier suffered three episodes of agonising stomach cramps. The last attack, on 22-23 March, proved fatal and he died at his lodgings. The post mortem revealed arsenic poisoning. There were 82 grains in his stomach alone.

Madeleine's sexually explicit letters - 198 of them - were found in L'Angelier's lodgings and in his office desk. She was arrested at the end of March.

Her trial lasted nine days. Summing up, the Lord Justice Clerk called Madeleine's letters "written without any sense of decency and in most licentious terms". But had she murdered L'Angelier?

The defence accepted she had bought arsenic on three occasions, but claimed there was no proof she'd met L'Angelier before any of the three instances when he became ill.

On 19 February 1857, William Minnoch took Madeleine to a performance of the opera "Lucrezia Borgia".

According to L'Angelier's diary, she met him later that evening. His diary entry reads:

*"**Saw Mimi** (his pet name for Madeleine) **a few moments, was very ill during the night.**"*

On 21 February, Madeleine bought arsenic from a Sauchiehall Street chemist. L'Angelier's diary entry for 22 February reads:

*"**Saw Mimi in drawing room. Promised me French Bible. Taken very ill.**"*

The diary was not allowed in evidence - and the jury was unaware of its contents.

On the evening of 22 March, when L'Angelier suffered his fatal attack, he was seen in Sauchiehall Street, heading towards Blythswood Square. He also called at a lodging house five minutes' walk from the square. At 2.30am on 23 March, he returned to his lodgings, in great agony. He died a few hours later. But the defence showed that while the arsenic bought by Madeleine Smith had been mixed with soot and waste indigo (it was legally required that it be mixed with colouring material) neither soot nor indigo was found in L'Angelier's stomach. Madeleine maintained she'd purchased arsenic for use as a cosmetic, diluted with water, for washing her face, neck and arms.

The all-male jury returned the verdict of not proven.

Prior to her notoriety, Madeleine Smith was photographed twice by a leading Glasgow photographer - once with members of her family and once on her own. While she was on trial, the photographer displayed in his shop window a large hand-coloured portrait of Madeleine Smith. Huge crowds formed outside the shop, blocking the street. Police were called to keep the thoroughfare clear.

Later, the photographer described Madeleine as "a strikingly beautiful girl". At her trial, however, a reporter described her face as "fox-like, unattractive, cunning, deceitful and altogether unprepossessing".

Madeleine Smith's engagement to William Minnoch ended, but she went on to marry twice. She died peacefully in New York in 1928, at the ripe old age of 92. She was buried as Lena Sheehy.

In the 1880s, while married to her first husband, an artist employed by leading radical William Morris, she became a socialist. George Bernard Shaw described her as "an ordinary, good-humoured, capable woman with nothing sinister about her".

Was Madeleine Smith "mad, bad and dangerous to know" - an emotional and sexual predator who coolly murdered a social inferior in order to make an advantageous middle-class Victorian marriage? Or was she a spirited and intelligent woman, trapped by "Victorian values"? Her later life - conversion to socialism, for example - suggests a person of independence and intelligence.

Public interest in Madeleine Smith remains intense. She'll feature in movies and museums for a very long time to come.

THE SANDYFORD PLACE MURDER

ONE of the most sinister exhibits in Strathclyde Police Museum is a footprint in blood, made on a wooden plank in July 1862. The footprint belonged to a young woman called Jessie McLachlan - convicted of the murder of servant girl Jessie McPherson.

Jessie McPherson was employed at 17 Sandyford Place, fronting Glasgow's Sauchiehall Street. The house was occupied by John Fleming, a prosperous accountant, his sister, son, two daughters, and John's 78-year-old father, James Fleming.

James Fleming began as a handloom weaver in Kilsyth, but made or saved enough money to move to Glasgow's Anderston, where he set up as a textiles manufacturer.

Fleming spoke broad Scots, and was an avid church-goer. He also had coarse manners and was more than fond of a dram. His family adopted genteel "city" codes of behaviour - and James embarrassed his *nouveau riche* brood. He was more at home below stairs than in the drawing room.

Hob-nobbing with household staff led him, in 1852, to appear before the kirk session, after fathering a child on a domestic servant. He might have had other opportunities to philander among vulnerable poor people, too. John Fleming paid his father £40 a year to collect rents on slum properties in Glasgow's deprived Briggait.

In common with many wealthy Glasgow families, the Flemings had a holiday villa in Dunoon. On July 4, 1862, they went to Dunoon, leaving James in charge at 17 Sandyford Place. They returned the following Monday afternoon. John Fleming's son was first to arrive at the house. The door wasn't opened as usual by the servant Jessie McPherson.

James answered the door.

"Where is Jessie?", asked John Fleming junior. His grandfather replied:

"She's away; she's cut. I haven't seen her since Friday, and her door's locked."

After John Fleming senior arrived, the three men descended to the basement. Using a spare key, they unlocked Jessie McPherson's bedroom.

She was lying practically naked on the floor, a piece of carpet covering her head. John Fleming senior rushed for a doctor, who rapidly decided this was no accident. Police were summoned.

A police surgeon found the young woman had been savagely attacked about the head and arms, apparently with an axe or cleaver. Her head was horribly mutilated. A trail of blood along the lobby between the kitchen and the bedroom revealed that Jessie McPherson's body had been dragged from one apartment to the other. Though the floors of the kitchen, lobby and bedroom were damp, and had evidently been recently washed, there were three footprints in blood near the woman's bed. Boards bearing the bloody footprints were removed for further examination.

The footprints were of the same naked foot - and not those of James Fleming or Jessie McPherson. There were other traces of blood in the basement, and in Fleming's room on the floor above. In a room used as a wardrobe by James Fleming, several of his spare shirts were spattered with blood. In a kitchen drawer, police found a butcher's cleaver. Several of the dead woman's dresses were missing. James Fleming reported that silver plate - forks, spoons and other items - had also disappeared.

The post-mortem on Jessie McPherson suggested:

"The comparatively light degree of strength shown in the blows would point to a female or a weak man having inflicted them."

Further investigation uncovered a witness in the form of dressmaker Mary McIntyre, who had heard a low wailing noise from 17 Sandyford Place as she passed by at about 11.45pm on Friday, July 4. She also noticed a light showing in the basement of the house. The following morning, at 4am, three girls returning from a dance noticed the gas light was still burning in the ground floor of 17 Sandyford Place. At 7.40am, a milk boy called - and the door was opened by James Fleming. Normally, that would have been Jessie McPherson's job.

James Fleming claimed he heard screams on the night of the murder and also admitted he'd noticed spots of blood on his spare shirts. He claimed also to have spent the entire weekend in the house, except for collecting rents and attending church. He said he'd met a number of people, including the milk boy, one of Jessie McPherson's male friends, some of his son's office staff, and fellow members of his kirk - which he'd attended twice on Sunday, July 6. Fleming stated he'd let himself in and out of the house, and cooked or brought in his meals - all apparently without wondering where his servant had gone or why her bedroom door was locked.

On July 28, a pawnbroker read about the missing plate and recalled that a woman had pledged similar articles on the previous Saturday. On July 29, he examined the plate, and found that every piece bore the letter "F". The plate had been pledged in the name of Mary McDonald, 5 St Vincent Street, Glasgow. He handed the items to the police, and described "Mary McDonald".

Later that day, James Fleming was arrested in connection with the murder of Jessie McPherson - and was remanded in custody. Acting on information apparently supplied by Fleming, police attention turned to Mrs Jessie McLachlan, 182 Broomielaw, Glasgow. A close friend of the dead woman, Mrs McLachlan had also been a servant in the Fleming household. Mrs McLachlan stated she'd last seen Jessie McPherson on the night of Saturday, June 28. She denied being in or near 17 Sandyford Place on July 4-5.

She claimed James Fleming called at her Broomielaw flat on the evening of Friday, July 4, with a parcel of silver plate - which he asked her to pawn for him as he was short of money. She pawned the plate the next day, using the name "McDonald", suggested by Fleming. He returned to claim the pawn ticket - and gave McLachlan £4 for her trouble.

McLachlan's story conflicted with the results of the police inquiry. She had been out of her house on the night of July 4-5. She'd gone out wearing an old dress and returned, according to her landlady, wearing one which her landlady hadn't seen before. Jessie Mclachlan was remanded in custody.

On July 16, Dr George Macleod, who'd examined the boards from the bedroom floor, brought to Mrs McLachlan several planks of wood, a piece of linoleum and a phial of bullock's blood. He smeared the blood on the linoleum, asked Mrs McLachlan to put her foot on it and obtained similar footprints using the wood. The experiment revealed that the prints corresponded to those found in Jessie McPherson's bedroom. Police also recovered clothes belonging to Jessie McPherson, which had been in Mrs McLachlan's possession.

By then convinced of Mrs McLachlan's guilt, the authorities released James Fleming. Jessie McLachlan was tried in Glasgow between 17 and 20 September, 1862. Unlike Madeleine Smith, who was given the courtesy of trial in Edinburgh, well away from the Glasgow press and popular opinion, Mrs McLachlan had to face trial in a city where the leading newspaper, *The Herald*, campaigned vociferously for James Fleming - calling him the "old innocent".

Witnesses testified that Jessie McPherson had complained of sexual harassment by James Fleming - calling him the "old devil".

Mary McIntyre said she'd seen Mrs McLachlan in a lane *outside* 17 Sandyford Place, seconds before she heard wailing noises coming from *inside* the house.

But, in Victorian Glasgow, Fleming's social status and apparent piety stood him in good stead. The child fathered on a previous servant was evidently overlooked. Even before the jury retired to consider its verdict, the judge ostentatiously displayed the black cap for all to see. The jury took only 15 minutes to return a unanimous verdict of guilty as charged.

But then, in one of the greatest sensations in Scottish legal history, Mrs McLachlan's agent read out a statement she had made to her lawyers on August 13, as soon as she had learned of James Fleming's release.

The statement claimed that, on the night of Friday, July 4, she had visited Jessie McLachlan. James Fleming had been present in the basement at 17 Sandyford Place, along with both women.

Fleming sent Mrs McLachlan to purchase whisky. When she returned, Jessie McPherson was on the floor, bleeding heavily from a wound on her forehead. Fleming told her he hadn't intended to hurt the servant - there had been an accident.

While Fleming was out of the room, Mrs McLachlan tended Jessie McPherson. Her statement claimed further that the injured woman told her about sexual approaches from Fleming - about two weeks previously.

In the early hours of the morning, Jessie McPherson's condition deteriorated. Fleming refused to open the locked door of the house to allow Mrs McLachlan to fetch a doctor. Mrs McLachlan then claimed that, at about 4am on July 5, while she was in the back parlour of 17 Sandyford Place, Fleming butchered the injured servant with a meat cleaver. Mrs McLachlan claimed Fleming then threatened her - saying that if she informed the police of what he'd done, he'd deny killing Jessie McPherson and would have her charged with the crime.

He then is alleged to have asked Mrs McLachlan to co-operate with him in simulating a burglary by removing some clothes and silver plate. Frightened and intimidated, she agreed.

While Mrs Mclachlan was still in the house, Fleming washed the basement floor and burned his blood-spattered shirt. The trial judge, Lord Deas - consistently hostile to Mrs McLachlan throughout the trial - refused to give any credence to her post-conviction statement. Deas stated he was convinced the "old gentleman" had nothing to do with the murder. He donned the black cap and passed sentence of death on Mrs McLachlan.

The Herald rejoiced at vindication of the "old innocent". Other papers - and public opinion - denounced the trial and verdict. Fifty thousand Glaswegians signed a petition to delay Mrs Mclachlan's execution. The sheriff who'd previously examined James Fleming - and found his behaviour after the murder "extremely suspicious" - said Mrs McLachlan had not received a fair trial:

"The minds of the jury were made up before they entered the box. Mrs McLachlan's statement bears the mark of truth, coincides in a remarkable way with the evidence, and explains much in the case which is otherwise inexplicable".

Medical pioneer Lord Lister concurred:

"The medical features of the tragedy are in remarkable accordance with the prisoner's statement."

Hostile demonstrations forced James Fleming to flee to his family's Dunoon villa. On November 6, 1862, after an official inquiry and a report to the Home Secretary, the death sentence on Mrs McLachlan was commuted to penal servitude for life. She served 15 years in prison, and was released on parole - then known as "ticket of leave" - in 1877.

She had been a model convict, but continued to proclaim her innocence of the Sandyford Place murder. Like Madeleine Smith, she went to the USA, where she died on January 1, 1899.

Was the conviction of Mrs Mclachlan an instance of "class vengeance masquerading as justice"? Was it an example of how "powerless" women can become when faced with sexual harassment and "power plays" by men? Or was Mrs McLachlan James Fleming's accomplice?

Policing in Glasgow was only 60 years old, and still working for full acceptance by the community. So, it's possible that Mrs McLachlan, in common with many working class people, might have felt that no-one would listen to her if she had gone to the police immediately after leaving 17 Sandyford Place on the night of July 4-5.

OSCAR SLATER

ON THE evening of December 21, 1908, elderly spinster Marion Gilchrist was brutally murdered in her flat in Glasgow's West Princes Street, during the temporary absence of her maid, who'd gone to buy an evening paper.

Arthur Adams, occupant of the flat below, was in his dining room with his sisters when he heard loud noises from above. He immediately went upstairs to investigate. He rang Miss Gilchrist's bell three times, without answer. He returned to his own flat, but the noises continued.

Adams went upstairs again. He was about to ring the bell when the maid, Helen Lambie, returned. She opened the door of her employer's flat and crossed the hall to the kitchen. As she did so, a well-dressed man emerged from the bedroom and passed Adams, who was still standing on the doorstep. Lambie also saw the man, but gave no indication that he might be an intruder. On reaching the landing, the man rushed downstairs.

In the dining room, the maid found Miss Gilchrist dying on the floor. She called out for Adams. He joined her and was horrified to see the body of the old lady lying in front of the fireplace with a rug over her head. Adams then ran into the street, but the mystery man had vanished.

Miss Gilchrist had been attacked with such ferocity that her face was smashed to pulp. Detectives arrived and searched the flat. In the bedroom, valuable jewellery lay on the toilet table. The wardrobe, containing £3000 worth of jewels, hidden by Miss Gilchrist among her dresses, was untouched. The mysterious visitor had only broken open a small box in which the deceased had kept her private papers, scattering its contents. Lambie, however, insisted that a diamond crescent brooch was missing.

The mystery man had used matches to light the bedroom gas, leaving his matchbox behind. He'd also handled the documents box and lamp bracket. A close-up photograph taken at the time revealed a bloody handprint on the back of one of the dining room chairs. In the back court, police found an auger with grey human hairs attached. Yet no fingerprint tests were carried out - although the process had been used in Glasgow for some years.

Adams was short-sighted, and hadn't been wearing his glasses when he encountered the intruder. But immediately after the murder, Lambie ran to the nearby home of Miss

Gilchrist's niece, Miss Margaret Birrell, and named the man who'd emerged from the bedroom. Lambie and Miss Birrell passed this information to the police, who duly interviewed the man in his house in Great Western Road, Glasgow.

During the subsequent trial of German-born Oscar Slater for killing Miss Gilchrist, Dr Francis Charteris, the man named by Lambie and Birrell, was referred to only as "A.B.". Charteris was a nephew of Miss Gilchrist.

On December 23, Mary Barrowman, a young message girl, gave a detailed description of a man who, she claimed, had run down the steps from Miss Gilchrist's close and rushed away.

On December 25, police issued descriptions of two men - the man seen by Lambie and Adams and the man seen by Mary Bowman. The previous day, a newspaper suggested robbery was not the motive for the killing:

"Documents of some kind, it is believed, were what the visitor was after and the probability is that for a day or two, at least, the police will pursue a keen investigation along that line."

On December 26, **The Herald** reported:

"Whatever way investigations are tending, it has been learned that the police have not departed from the opinion that the assailant was already known to the victim."

Miss Gilchrist's father had left her a substantial fortune. She was on bad terms with her wider family - which included three sisters and a number of nephews.

The theory that two men were involved in Miss Gilchrist's murder was reinforced by new evidence. On December 31, Agnes Brown, a schoolteacher, stated she had seen two well-dressed men running away from the scene of the crime.

On the evening of December 25, Allan McLean, a cycle dealer, told police that a German Jew, whom he knew only as "Oscar", had been trying to sell a pawn ticket for a diamond brooch resembling the missing item. McLean accompanied an officer to St George's Mansions, near Glasgow's Sauchiehall Street, and pointed out the close where "Oscar" lived. Inquiries revealed the flat was rented in the name of "Anderson". At midnight, steps were taken to arrest "Oscar". But by then he'd left for Liverpool, accompanied by a lady friend.

The man on whom police now fixed their attention was Oscar Slater - a member of several Glasgow gambling clubs. The brooch he'd pawned was traced to a Sauchiehall Street pawnshop - pledged a month before the murder.

Although police now had nothing to connect Slater with the murder of Miss Gilchrist, they pursued him to New York, where he was "identified" by the witnesses Lambie and Barrowman. Slater had openly discussed his plans to leave Glasgow for America, a country he'd visited several times before. On arrival in Liverpool, he registered as "Oscar Slater, Glasgow" - hardly the action of a man on the run. For domestic reasons in both London and Glasgow, years before the West Princes Street murder, he'd used the name "Adolf

Anderson". Slater was a married man but cohabited with a girlfriend. Without waiting for extradition proceedings, and anxious to clear his name, Slater voluntarily returned to Scotland.

One man believed Oscar Slater had nothing to do with the murder of Miss Gilchrist. John Thomson Trench, a detective-lieutenant in the City of Glasgow Police, believed Slater had nothing to do with the murder. Two days after the killing, Trench was instructed to interview Miss Birrell and take her statement. From that moment, Trench's future was intertwined with the fate of Oscar Slater.

According to Miss Birrell, Helen Lambie had identified the mystery man as Dr Francis Charteris. Trench delivered the statement to his superior officer, Chief Superintendent Orr, who remarked: "This is the first clue we have got." Trench was informed that Charteris "had nothing to do with it" - and was ordered to return to Miss Birrell and warn her not to repeat Lambie's claims.

Oscar Slater's trial began in the High Court at Edinburgh on May 3, 1909. One of the most important exhibits was a tiny hammer, found in Slater's luggage. The Crown alleged it was the murder weapon, although the doctor who'd first examined Miss Gilchrist's body had noticed that the leg of one of the dining room chairs was "dripping" with blood - and the auger with grey human hairs remained unexplained. The chair was not produced at Oscar Slater's trial.

Much weight was given to Mary Barrowman's confident "identification" of the man she'd seen on 23 December, 1908. Not surpisingly, the prosecution didn't call Agnes Brown - who claimed to have seen two men running from the murder locus. All major prosecution witnesses said the man they'd seen was clean shaven. Oscar Slater had a prominent moustache.

The jury took 70 minutes to consider its verdict. The vote was: guilty, 9; not proven, 5; not guilty, 1.

Oscar Slater was set down for execution in Glasgow on May 27, 1909. If he had been in England and Wales, he could have turned to the then recently established Court of Criminal Appeal, but in 1908, no such body existed in Scotland. A petition seeking commutation of his sentence attracted more than 20,000 signatures. On the eve of execution, his sentence was commuted to penal servitude for life. In view of the heinous nature of the crime, it is not clear why a reprieve was granted - unless higher authorities were not entirely convinced of Slater's guilt.

John Trench, who'd joined the City of Glasgow Police as a constable in 1893, became a lieutenant in 1912, and held the King's Police Medal. He firmly believed Slater's conviction was unsound. In 1914, he consulted a lawyer - who believed Trench's story and advised him to tell it. Trench sought assurances from the Secretary of State for Scotland that he would not suffer if he acted in accordance with his conscience. The Secretary of State asked Trench to send a written statement of the evidence in his possession. Trench complied, and the Secretary of State for Scotland duly announced the appointment of the Sheriff of Lanarkshire to head an inquiry into the case of Oscar Slater.

Sir Arthur Conan Doyle, creator of Sherlock Holmes, and a strong believer in Slater's innocence, wrote:

"The police are as much on trial as Slater. If the methods of the police are not to be investigated the inquiry is futile."

The inquiry was held in camera, witnesses were not compelled to appear, and they were not examined on oath.

Helen Lambie denied she'd identified the man in the house as Dr Charteris. So did Miss Birrell. Slater's conviction was upheld. On September 14, 1914, Lt Trench was dismissed from the City of Glasgow Police "for communicating to persons outside the police force information he had acquired in the course of his duty". He appealed to the Secretary of State for Scotland. There was no reply.

Trench, who forfeited his pension rights after 21 years' service, served in France and Egypt during WW1. He died in 1919.

In 1925, Slater smuggled a letter out of Peterhead prison, addressed to Sir Arthur Conan Doyle, pleading for him to make a last attempt to secure Slater's release. Slater had already served 15 years.

Sir Arthur wrote to the Secretary of State for Scotland, but was rebuffed. Two years later, Glasgow journalist William Park published *The Truth About Oscar Slater*. The book renewed controversy over the 1909 conviction. Crime novelist Edgar Wallace claimed Helen Lambie knew the real murderer:

"Obviously she knew him; as obviously, to my mind, the murderer was in the house when she left. Nothing was said about the blood-stained chair, because it did not fit the case which had been manufactured against Oscar Slater."

In 1927, a newspaper interviewed Helen Lambie, who'd emigrated to America. She admitted she knew the man in the flat as a person who regularly visited her mistress. She claimed she told the police of this, but was advised it was nonsense. She claimed police persuaded her she was mistaken. According to Lambie, the man was not unlike Slater, but was better dressed and of higher social station.

Another paper tracked down Mary Barrowman, who said that in identifying Slater she meant he was "like" the man who'd collided with her on the night of the murder. She claimed the procurator fiscal bullied her into saying Slater was the man involved.

On November 14, 1927, Oscar Slater was released on licence. In 1928, a special Court of Appeal quashed his conviction, on a point of law. He received £6000 compensation. He died in 1948. Ironically, as an unnaturalised alien, he was interned at the beginning of WW2.

Shortly before his own death, Sir Arthur Conan Doyle wrote to criminologist William Roughead:

"I think that when A.B. dies a flood of evidence may come out. I think, also, that when Helen Lambie dies she may leave a full confession. Only along these lines do I see any hope of clearing the mystery."

Helen Lambie eventually returned to the UK. She never made that "full confession". Dr Francis Charteris died in 1964. His secrets went with him to the grave.

It's been claimed the two men in Miss Gilchrist's flat were Charteris and and Wingate Birrell, another of Miss Gilchrist's nephews. Supposedly, yet another nephew kept watch in the street. They're supposed to have been searching for Miss Gilchrist's will, which she had allegedly altered to the detriment of her relations.

That's as plausible as any other theory - and there have been many. But no evidence has been produced to prove that Wingate Birrell was in Glasgow in 1908. Miss Gilchrist's killer remains to be identified.

Supporters of Scotland's "not proven" verdict claim it protects probably innocent people from concerted "frame-ups" on the Oscar Slater model. Opponents damn the verdict as a "rogues' charter". At first glance, it would seem to have allowed the likes of Madeleine Smith to escape the ultimate penalty for their crimes.

Victorian and Edwardian murders in Scotland reveal - often graphically - the nature of that society. As illustrated by the example of James Fleming, alcohol abuse and illicit sexuality could flourish side by side with public religious piety.

Many people, high or low - such as Sir Arthur Conan Doyle or the thousands of Glaswegians who tried to save Jessie McLachlan - were prepared to challenge authority's decisions and actions. Thousands more were content to uncritically accept society's structures and ethos.

Could such injustices happen today? The answer has to be "not proven". ☐

UNDER THE MICROSCOPE

I N STRATHCLYDE Police Museum, the outline of a foot traced in blood on a board dating from 1862 represents an early attempt at something approaching modern forensic science in the service of fighting and detecting crime. Following the murder of Victorian servant girl Jessie McPherson, a doctor went to suspect Jessie McLachlan in Glasgow's Duke Street jail, carrying some wooden boards and a quantity of bullocks' blood.

Object of the exercise was to find out whether or not Mrs McLachlan's foot, once dipped in blood, matched a bloody footprint found at the murder scene. It did.

The notorious Sandyford Place murder, covered elsewhere in this book, remains one of the West of Scotland's much debated "unsolved mysteries". But the instance of the bloody foot revealed that 150 years ago science was emerging rapidly as a servant of policing and criminal justice.

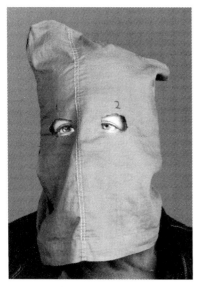

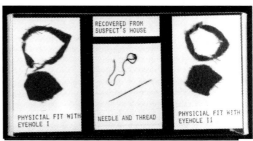

This hood was worn by a robber in Strathclyde. In his house police found discarded pieces of cloth cut out to make eyeholes. Forensic examination revealed a precise physical fit between the fragments found in the house and the mask worn during the robbery

In the late 1990s, Strathclyde Police Forensic Science Laboratory employs 55 people - and also works on behalf of other forces throughout Scotland.

The service was founded by reforming chief constable Percy Sillitoe. The laboratory, originally staffed by police officers, was established within the City of Glasgow Police Identification Bureau in 1943. Civilianisation began in 1965. In 1988, the laboratory was comprehensively expanded and refurbished.

In 1995 alone, scientists gave evidence in court on 250 occasions. In 1997, scientists gave evidence in court on 160 occasions. During 1997-98, the laboratory dealt with

9763 cases, including 5214 drugs cases and 606 blood and urine alcohol analyses under the terms of the Road Traffic Offenders Act.

Close liaison is maintained with other Scottish police forces - for whom the Strathclyde laboratory provides services such as DNA profiling, tachograph analyses and tyre examinations.

Strathclyde Police Forensic Science Laboratory's late-20th century mission statement reflects its founding ethos:

"To support impartially the administration of justice by providing a total quality forensic science service from within Strathclyde Police".

Staff are professional scientists. Their worth to society depends on courts, lawyers, press, politicians and public accepting that their evidence is based on scientific principles of integrity, honesty and independence. Police scientists do not "obtain convictions". They provide facts. As citizens, staff might have their own ideas about the guilt or otherwise of a suspect in a particular case. The professional task is to present evidence. Judges and juries convict people. The laboratory made very clear its role in the 1990s:

"The main aim of the department is to provide impartial and confidential scientific advice and support to enhance delivery of justice whilst simultaneously consolidating our reputation for openness and integrity."

Forensic science is constrained by the amount of evidence left at the scene of a crime, the state of technology, and willingness of courts and juries to accept technical and scientific evidence. Forensic science involves painstaking organisation, departmental and individual discipline, and constant awareness of the need for scientific, corporate and individual integrity and credibility.

Elsewhere in the UK, adverse publicity from a few high-profile cases left forensic science services facing the task of rebuilding public and professional confidence. Very little such criticism has involved forensic science services in Scotland.

While a great deal of the Strathclyde laboratory's work is of a routine nature, staff have been involved in many dramatic - and occasionally disturbing - investigations. In 1995, the body of 16-year-old Mhairi Julyan was found within Kilmarnock's main bus garage. Almost immediately, tread plates were laid down - ensuring footwear impressions were not destroyed.

The girl's body was found in a bunker. Her bra had been used as a gag. The sleeves of her blouse had been tied at the back of her head and used as a ligature. Among items recovered from the scene were a broken shoe lace, a large amount of debris, and soil from the victim's boots.

Elsewhere in the garage, there was found a mound of earth similar to that found on the girl's boots. Two hairs were also found and presented as a good match to her hair.

Most of the blood located came from Mhairi Julyan. But painstaking examination revealed a small bloodstain on her clothing which turned out to be a mixture of her blood and that of a then unknown male. There was similar blood on the section of lace found near the bunker.

DNA was extracted from all suspects' blood samples and compared with the unknown male's profile. The profile matched that received from a man named Gavin McGuire. Previous examination of suspects' clothing, including that belonging to McGuire, had revealed no traces of blood.

Forensic scientists also found coloured cotton fibres - later found to be indistinguishable from a shirt worn by McGuire at the time of the incident.

At the time of the murder of Mhairi Julyan, McGuire lived at his mother's home. There, a single white lace was found in a kitchen drawer - and was indistinguishable in construction detail to the piece of lace found at the locus. Laces from six pairs of sandshoes found at the accused's mother's house were also examined - and found to be indistinguishable from the lace in the drawer and at the murder scene. But - underlining the "real life" dilemmas and problems facing forensic scientists - it was not possible to determine how common such laces were.

A jury found Gavin McGuire guilty of killing Mhairi Julyan. Lord Clyde recommended he serve at least 30 years in prison.

Strathclyde Police Museum features also a tiny piece of metal found in 1987 embedded in the wrist bone of the owner of a Chinese restaurant in Glasgow. He had been attacked by knife-wielding members of a so-called "Triad" gang - a movement alleged to extort "protection money" from ethnic minority business operators throughout the UK, as well as being involved in moneylending, drug trading and organised prostitution. He had been struck on the arm by knife blows.

It has been notoriously difficult for police throughout the UK to bring Triad gangs to book. Scotland's Chinese community is very small, and although considerable efforts have been made to assist Chinese people to integrate with and benefit from the wider host society - many older Chinese people have serious language difficulties and remain strongly located within their own "mini culture". This - combined with understandable determination on the part of Chinese people to retain their small community in the face of racism and other forms of hostility in their new country - makes gathering criminal intelligence on Triads a particularly difficult task.

For some months, it appeared that the Glasgow attack might never be solved. Then, members of a Triad gang were caught in another crime in Nottingham. One of the arrested men was found in possession of a large knife - with a piece of metal missing from the blade. Forensic examination revealed that the metal fragment lodged in the wrist of the Glasgow restaurateur fitted precisely into the blade of the Nottingham knife. A conviction followed.

The House of Commons Select Committee on Science and Technology has praised the work of police forensic scientists:

"It is a highly cost-effective element of the criminal justice system".

Emphases on quality, integrity and professional independence have been reinforced by the committee's findings. But the MPs warned:

"However, the recent spate of collapsed convictions has precipitated a crisis of confidence and left forensic science with an image problem."

Such warnings are apposite and plain enough. Forensic scientists can go from "heroes" to "stitch-up merchants" in public perception - apparently almost overnight. Late-20th century restatements of scientific ethics and independence are a contribution by forensic science in Strathclyde to the permanent recognition that policing - in all its aspects - rests on public support and assent. As police officers are "citizens in uniform", so forensic scientists are "citizens with microscopes". ☐

THE DICED CAP

IN 1778, when Glasgow Town Council established a short-lived police force, ex-bailie Richard Marshall was appointed Intendant of Police and provided with a white rod and a gold chain of office. His force of eight men wore quasi-military red coats.

Citizens disliked such "military style" - and in 1800, when Glasgow established its permanent police force, sergeants and other senior ranks were provided with civilian-style blue coats, vests and knee breeches. Rank and file officers were issued with greatcoats. Each man's number was painted on the back of his coat.

Swallow-tail coats of the 1800s gave way in the 1840s to knee-length, wide skirted tunics, closed at the neck, resembling Victorian frock coats. Insignia on early uniforms consisted of letters and numerals embroidered on the high "choker" collars of tunics.

By 1870, many forces issued close-fitting military-style tunics. Senior police officers wore heavily frogged and braided frock coats. Leather belts, worn over tunics, provided a place for officers to hang their "bull's eye" oil lamps.

By the 1880s, the Secretary of State for Scotland permitted many forces (mostly county constabularies) to adopt "patrol uniforms" and forage caps rather than helmets. The mounted sergeant featured in the museum illustrates this change.

Forage caps were the forerunner of peaked caps - referred to by PCs as "the German jammer", from supposed resemblance to German military headwear. The years 1948-50 brought the end of closed-neck jackets. By the 1950s, police officers were allowed to appear in "shirt-sleeve order". The movement to more relaxed uniforms was aided by post-WW2 development of lighter-weight fabrics and self-supporting trousers.

Until the 1860s, constables wore civilian-style glazed tall hats - the "stovepipe" or "lum" hats worn by upper-class men during the 19th century. Most officers were recruited from the ranks of working men - who normally wore bonnets or cloth caps. Lum hats gave constables a touch of *gravitas* as they patrolled urban Scotland's less salubrious industrial areas.

By the 1870s, many forces had adopted domed helmets. As with new-style tunics, helmets were military in style, and resembled helmets worn by many units of the Volunteer movement - forerunners of the Territorial Army. This was not a return to military-style uniforms per se. The Volunteer movement was popular, widespread - and classless.

Many forces adopted helmets topped with ornate ventilation pieces in the form of spikes, globes or rosettes.

In the 19th century, local patriotism was a powerful force in Scotland, and helmet badges often reflected local industries or emblems. The badge of Greenock Burgh Police depicted a clipper ship - a link with the town's long sea-faring traditions.

In 1906, Paisley Burgh Police obtained Army-surplus slouch hats. The hats were dyed blue for police use. It is said that when it rained, dye ran down down officers' faces.

Pressure to end wearing of helmets by Scottish police forces first surfaced in the 1880s and was vocal by the 1930s. In 1934, *The Herald* reported:

"The joint central committee of the Scottish Police Federation, after considering proposals for alterations in police uniforms, suggests that for sergeants and constables the helmet should be abolished, and that uniform caps should be the recognised standard throughout Scotland."

Straw helmets for summer use were issued to Kilmarnock Burgh Police - and were worn as late as the 1940's.

Badge of Maryhill Burgh Police prior to amalamation with Glasgow. The badge depicts pioneer steamship Charlotte Dundas crossing Skaethorn Viaduct on the Forth and Clyde Canal

By the late 1930s, increasing use of cars by police forces encouraged adoption of flat caps. Some Scottish police forces, including Argyllshire and Lanarkshire, wore white tops on their flat caps to distinguish officers from other uniformed officials.

After WW2, Scottish police forces abandoned helmets in favour of flat caps with black and white diced bands - the "Sillitoe tartan". Percy Sillitoe, Glasgow's chief constable between 1932 and 1943, is supposed to have based the design on the cap band worn by the Scots Guards. Diced caps are now increasingly worn by police forces throughout the world. Evolution of the black and white chequered band is illustrated in Strathclyde Police Museum.

Victorian police officers wore uniform on or off duty. "Duty bands" - blue and white striped armlets worn on the left cuff - were introduced in the 1830s.

41

Prior to introduction of warrant cards, police officers carried tipstaffs for identification purposes. Tipstaffs, or tipstaves, were originally wooden staffs or staves with metal tips.

Dumbarton Burgh Police badge with
"Elephant and Castle" civic emblem

Govan Burgh Police badge with
shipbuilding motif in centre.

These were carried by officials as symbols of authority under the Crown. Police tipstaffs were about six inches long and made of brass or wood. Tips were usually finished with a crown. Many older tipstaffs were hollow, usually unscrewing at the crown. Tipstaffs were expensive to produce and were replaced by warrant cards in the late-19th century. To this day, however, shoulder insignia worn by chief police officers in Scotland consists of crossed tipstaves in a thistle leaf wreath.

In 1800, when the City of Glasgow Police was founded, officers carried long sticks - to extinguish street lamps as well as for personal protection. Batons or truncheons were adopted by most forces at an early stage in their development. Firearms and swords were issued only in unusual circumstances - as during both world wars, when officers guarding vital installations were armed with revolvers.

In 1819, the Burgh of Calton - then on the eastern fringe of the city of Glasgow - established a police force. Calton, largely inhabited by poverty-stricken weavers, was considered a particularly lawless place. Constables patrolled in pairs, and carried both sticks and cutlasses. Such weapons were used to good effect when two constables surprised a gang of body snatchers in the act of removing a corpse from a grave in Calton burying ground. One of the grave robbers had an arm almost severed by a cutlass blow.

Early batons were usually about 20 inches long, and were made of hardwoods such as teak or ebony. They were often decorated with coats of arms and the VR cipher.

Over time, batons became smaller, and shapes were altered - original cylinder-style batons became tapered, with a series of rings for gripping the handle. Initially, truncheons were carried in tailcoats. Later, they were carried on the right-hand side of belts, and eventually were carried in specially made trouser pockets. A baton scabbard is displayed in the museum.

Prior to introduction of efficient handcuffs, officers held prisoners with "snitchers" - simple rope ties with wooden handles. This could be the origin of the term "snitch".

Metal handcuffs came into use comparatively early in police history, and by the mid-19th century Birmingham-based Hiatt and Co supplied handcuffs to most UK forces. The company still supplies handcuffs to Strathclyde Police.

An Ayrshire constable c.1912. Prior to WW1, officers had to rely on bulky "bullseye" lanterns.

In WW1, electric torches were developed for use in trench warfare - and rapidly became standard equipment in civil society after cessation of hostilities.

Police officers who served in large numbers in WW1 would have been well aware of the value of such innovations in fighting crime rather than the Kaiser.

Police in Springburn, Glasgow, used unusual "figure of eight" handcuffs. One section locked onto a prisoner's wrist, while the other section was held by the escort. Most common type was D-shaped handcuffs, fastened in the centre with a small chain. These were locked individually on each side by means of a key. They remained standard issue until replaced with lightweight snap-on ratchet-type handcuffs during the late-1960s.

For night duty in 1800, Glasgow's watchmen were equipped with lanterns, and each officer had two tallow candles - one for immediate use, the other a spare.

First electric lantern for police use was developed in the 1920s, by the Metropolitan Police. By the 1940s, lamps using dry batteries were in widespread use.

As motor traffic increased during the inter-war years, with consequent danger to officers on point duty, officers were equipped with white gloves and coats. During WW2, lighting restrictions placed officers in even greater danger. The City of Glasgow Police experimented with illuminated helmets. It seems the helmets were never used. A rare surviving example is in Strathclyde Police Museum. Early forces wore uniforms which were demonstrably not military in style. But during WW2, officers were issued with steel helmets and gas masks.

Some commentators have argued that prolonged police involvement in anti-terrorist activities with the Army in Northern Ireland has led to "militarisation" of police uniforms and equipment - creating so-called "techno-police". Such interpretations suggest that specialist firearms teams can appear as "commandos" - basing their uniforms and personal equipment on items issued to special forces.◻

"CODE 21 RED"

I N THE fight against crime in the 18th and early 19th centuries, handbills and newspaper advertisements were invaluable. In 1772, Glasgow magistrates advertised five guineas reward for information leading to the arrest of the person or persons who'd smashed a street lamp on Victoria Bridge - and offered 10 guineas reward for the capture of eight escapees from the city's Tolbooth.

In 1805, £5 was offered for the apprehension of Andrew Thomson, poacher, accused of shooting partridges on an estate near Glasgow:

"Thomson is little more than twenty years of age, rather tall and of a fair complexion, wore a fustian jacket and corduroy breeches; had a game bag under his jacket, carried a double barrelled gun, and hunted with a large brown and white pointer, very lean."

In the era before cheap mass-produced clothing, people could be identified by their dress. Often, the clothes they wore were all the garments they possessed. Many people also wore distinctive occupational clothing. Scottish towns were small, and strangers conspicuous.

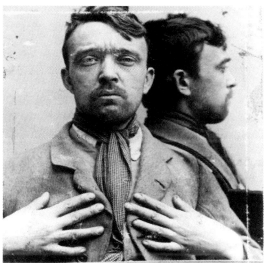

By the 1860s, many forces used photography to disseminate information about known criminals. Some early books of "mugshots" are displayed in the museum. Photography was first used to identify criminals on "ticket of leave" from prison on licence. Record books containing "mugshots" were held at police stations, along with details of convictions. Photographs often depicted both hands and faces of criminals, since in the days of heavy physical labour many individuals suffered distinctive injuries to their hands. Such records enabled beat constables to watch out for such people while on patrol. Pickpockets, for example, frequently haunted railway stations, race courses and street markets.

As formal policing emerged during the early 19th century, constables needed to communicate with colleagues. For much of the century, wooden rattles and clappers were the only resource for constables requiring help from other officers in their vicinity. These devices gave rise to the term "run like the clappers". Clappers could fit easily into officers' pockets. Rattles were more cumbersome, although some folding models were introduced.

A set of clappers in Strathclyde Police Museum

Police had to be sparing in their use of rattles. Victorian townspeople, especially millworkers and factory hands, began work very early - and objected to being disturbed at night. In 1883, experiments in London found that rattles could be clearly heard up to 400 yards. Whistles carried for up to 900 yards. By the end of the 19th century, most forces had adopted whistles. In the early 20th century, "pea whistles" were largely replaced by air whistles, which remained in use until introduction of personal radios during the 1960s.

Turnpike roads, fast coaches and the growth of railways made criminals more mobile. In the mid-19th century, a Glasgow shebeener described stocking gin and champagne for "English thieves" in the city. In 1844, a Liverpudlian - "dressed in the very pink of fashion" - picked a lady's pocket in Glasgow's Buchanan Street. In the same year, a gentleman travelling first-class from Edinburgh to Glasgow had his gold cravat pin filched when the train entered the tunnel at Glasgow's Queen Street station.

By the 1860s, the electric telegraph allowed descriptions of such criminals to be circulated faster than before. The City of Glasgow Police was among the first forces to introduce telegraph links between force HQ and outlying city stations. The ABC machine, patented in 1858, was comparatively simple to operate, and a skilled operator could attain speeds of 20-30 words per minute.

Ambitious police officers were advised to become proficient in use of the telegraph - supposed to be an *open sesame* to promotion.

Police forces quickly utilised the rapid advent of telephone systems. In 1886, the American city of Boston established a system of police boxes. By 1888, iron "street call boxes" equipped with telephones were installed in Islington, London.

Prior to introduction of police boxes, officers had to leave their beats to escort prisoners to a police station. Boxes allowed constables to summon police vehicles and continue patrolling. In 1891, a number of cast iron police boxes were installed in Glasgow. Each box contained a telephone and was surmounted by a gas lamp.

By 1914, there were 56 police signal boxes in Glasgow, linked by telephone to divisional police offices.by the early 1930s, police boxes of a new type were installed throughout the UK. These "miniature police stations" contained, in addition to telephones, stools, cupboards, desks and drawers, police box diaries, first aid kits, fire extinguishers and electric heaters. Telephones allowed officers to contact divisional stations at regular intervals. Signal lamps on top of the boxes alerted officers when station officers wished to contact them.

Police box in use after WW2. Although disused, surviving examples of police boxes can be seen in and around Glasgow.

Only police officers could enter the boxes, using special keys. Members of the public could use amplified two-way speakers, accessed from outside the boxes, to report suspicious incidents, make inquiries or obtain advice. Such use alerted beat constables by automatically triggering the red signal lights on top of the boxes.

The City of Glasgow Police began installing new pattern police boxes in 1933, starting with Bridgeton in the city's East End - the stamping ground of several notorious gangs. Red-painted boxes were usually erected at important street intersections where two or more beats converged. By 1939, there were 356 boxes in the city, in addition to 12 red-painted telephone pillars. Blue boxes were introduced in the 1970s.

The police box system improved co-operation between police and public. In 1937, Glasgow citizens made 2233 calls from police boxes. The system continued as a mainstay of police communications until the 1960s, when panda cars, personal radios, and rising maintenance costs made the miniature police stations obsolete. By the end of 1988, only 11 boxes remained in operation in Glasgow - mostly in the city centre.

By the mid-1920s, Scotland Yard was investigating the possible use of radio - then referred to as "wireless" - in the detection of crime. In a 1923 experiment, listeners to the then new BBC were given descriptions of "three villains loose in London in cars". One of the "guinea pigs" was identified and "captured" within minutes of the broadcast.

By the late 1920s, the Metropolitan Police Flying Squad had two vans equipped with wireless - using Morse Code. Operators had to wear headphones.

Interior of Glasgow's first radio-equiped police van.

In 1932, *The Herald* reported:

"A demonstration of the advantages of wireless communication in police work was given yesterday at the headquarters of Glasgow Police to chief constables and

representatives of several Scottish county and burgh forces. Mr P J Sillitoe, chief constable of Glasgow said:

"We propose to plot out the city for motor car patrols. These will operate during the evening and night-time. It would be my intention when the transmitter is working that the cars in the different areas allocated to them would be in constant touch with headquarters."

In 1933, *The Herald* also reported:

"The need for rapid communications and greater police mobility to combat the motor bandit is urged in the annual report of Brigadier General Dudgeon, HM Inspector of Constabulary in Scotland. The inspector also recommends the installation of wireless apparatus in patrol cars, the police box system and automatic traffic control."

He also suggested that the largest force in any particular area of Scotland should become the transmitting centre - and urged that Glasgow and Edinburgh be allowed to experiment with radio communications.

In 1934, the City of Glasgow Police rented a gatehouse at Glasgow Corporation's Pinkston Road power station. An aerial was installed on a 263ft-high chimney. Transmissions were initiated in March 1935, following test transmissions using a transmitter on loan from the RAF. In April 1935, speech transmissions were made to police headquarters at a number of locations throughout West and South-west Scotland.

In August 1935, six Glasgow police cars were equipped with receivers. These worked well - although officers had to ensure their vehicles were some distance from city trams whose non-suppressed electrical systems interfered with reception. In the same year, police boxes were used as radio centres during important events in Glasgow, such as VIP visits and sporting fixtures.

By 1936, police radio systems could reach stations and vehicles within 35 miles of Glasgow, and 29 vehicles had been equipped with receivers. Chief Constable Sillitoe attributed 66 arrests to use of radio - including 21 car thefts and 17 housebreakings.

Radio began to give policing a "Strathclyde" dimension. In Helensburgh, a patrolling constable apprehended a suspected housebreaker and was threatened by a hostile crowd. He telephoned his HQ, who in turn contacted the City of Glasgow Police. The Glasgow control room radioed to Dunbartonshire police vehicles. Praising the new system in his annual report, Sillitoe summarised the outcome.

"Assistance required. CID car and two patrol cars directed to locus. Services rendered. Situation brought under control and prisoner conveyed to station."

In his report for 1937, Sillitoe attributed 277 arrests to use of radio.

In December 1937, growing use of police radio equipment proved its worth in the aftermath of one of Scotland's worst rail disasters, at Castlecary, near Cumbernauld, when 35 people were killed and many more injured. The Scottish Ambulance Service sought assistance from the City of Glasgow Police in order to rapidly call out off duty staff. Radio enabled police vehicles to be quickly sent to the homes of ambulance staff. As ambulances from the crash scene headed for hospitals in Glasgow, radio-equipped cars stationed on the A80 directed them to appropriate hospitals - avoiding overloading of emergency facilities. Contemporary reports suggest that a number of lives were saved by this facility. Radio also enabled police to quickly contact relatives of the dead and injured.

Also in 1937, Sillitoe reported the ordering of police cars specially modified to accommodate radio apparatus - probably the first cars in the UK specially built for police purposes.

Police officers in Brighton were equipped with "pocket radios" as early as 1933 - but receivers and earphones weighed 4lbs. The sets, which only received messages, had a range of about six miles. It was not until the mid-1960s, with the advent of transistors, that personal radios, putting beat officers into instant communication with control rooms, were successfully introduced. Two-way personal radios were pioneered in 1964 in Glasgow's Pollok area.

Radio and telecommunications technology has developed quickly. In the early 21st century, police forces are likely to utilise the "Public Safety Radio Communications Project" (PSRCP) - being developed through the Police Information Technology Organisation (PITO) with input from all forces in the UK. At 1998 prices, PSRCP has been estimated to cost £1.5 billion. It could be operational in the Strathclyde Police area in the year 2004.

PSRCP could incorporate fire and ambulance services, HM Customs and Excise, HM Coastguard, Department of Transport and the Vehicle Inspectorate. The system is being developed as a response to criminal scanning - and scanning by unscrupulous sections of the media. Such electronic eavesdropping can frustrate delicate operations.

PSRCP will utilise digital trunk technology - ensuring encryption for all users. Current scanning technology will be rendered ineffective. The system will allow officers to access the Police National Computer (PNC) and the Scottish Criminal Record Office (SCRO) from operational vehicles, without their having to ask base controllers to do this for them. It will be possible for short text messages to be relayed to controllers without use of voice communication. A controller could dispatch officers to an incident, the officers could report their time of arrival, deal with the incident, update the controller and confirm that they were clear to attend a further call - all without a word being spoken on air.

PSRCP will also permit transmission of images - with photographs of accused persons being sent to officers on patrol for identification. Video and fax transmissions will also be possible. Officers attending an incident could relay video footage to their control - with commanders thus able to assess the seriousness of a situation.

Automatic location of vehicles and foot patrols will be a feature of the new system - enabling controllers to know where units are when actioning calls. Digital technology will diminish background noise, thus enhancing communication.

It is hoped PSRCP will become operational in Scotland in the early 21st century - part of a linear development which began with whistles, clappers, handbills, posters - and "polis boxes".

Use of computers to enhance communications - by providing accurate and rapid access to fingerprint files, criminal records and other aspects of police intelligence dates from 1988 - when the Scottish Criminal Record Office, created from archives held by individual forces throughout the country, ended the use of paper records. In the 1990s, computerised records, quickly accessible through networked personal computers in police offices, can provide operational officers with details of suspects which include convictions, pending cases, full descriptions of individuals and their modus operandi, and details of releases from prisons.

Since 1991, officers throughout Scotland have been supported by the Automatic Fingerprint Recognition System (AFR). AFR allows searches to be made for what are known as "10-print collections" in matter of a few hours. Prior to computerisation, very large numbers of police and civilian staff were needed to search manual records. The scale of that task can be gauged from the fact that, by 1998, there were 3,600,000 human fingers recorded on the Scottish Criminal Record Office system. In 1998, Scotland's entire criminal record staff comprised only 17 police officers and 83 civilians.

Fingerprint experts are highly skilled. Qualification takes five years, and staff must be at least 25 years old to be approved as expert witnesses.

In 1996, photographs were added to the system - greatly assisting identification of suspects. Members of the public no longer have to plough through books of "mugshots" - such as the 19th-century examples displayed in Strathclyde Police Museum. The advent of laptop computers means photographs can be taken to someone in hospital, for example. As the 21st century approaches, police officers are beginning to use digital cameras to capture "mugshots" - with resulting images fed directly into computer systems.

SCRO officers have worked with Glasgow University's Turin Institute on creating "facial mapping" and three-dimensional images - developments which might allow witnesses to "view" possible suspects from the angle at which they were observed during incidents, such as lying on the ground.

In 1997, police in Scotland began to deploy so-called "live scan" fingerprinting systems, in which human digits are read by machine and immediately filed electronically. Future developments might involve electronic capture of palm prints.

Development of communications reveals that policing has always been at the forefront of technology in society. That movement has always been controversial. Citizens captured on glass negatives by Victorian police photographers doubtless resented the innovation - which they might have damned as "takin bluidy liberties". Equally, their victims were probably only too glad to be able to identify their assailants. Two centuries of evolving policing technology simply underline the debate that constantly surrounds the profession. To some, computers and digital radio are tools of oppression. For others, they're safeguards of citizens' rights. The same probably went for handbills and whistles.◻

STRATHCLYDE AGAINST DRUGS

STRATHCLYDE Police Museum contains a section showing illegal drugs used in the West of Scotland - with an account of their constituents and effects. The museum also displays drugs-related artefacts including opium and cannabis pipes. Stimulants and narcotics are as old as civilisation. They've been prohibited in some societies - exalted in others. The term "cannabis" stems from the Greek word "kannabis". Early Sumerian writings refer to "ka na ba".

Farming historians suggest hemp - the plant which produces cannabis - has been cultivated for perhaps 10,000 years. Earliest known fabrics were woven from hemp. Ancient Indian texts list hemp among the "five sacred kingdoms of herbs". Ancient Native Americans also used hemp - along with approximately 40 other known hallucinogens. The name Bangladesh translates as "Land of the Hemp People". Ancient Greek historian Herodotus refers to Central European peoples growing hemp and using cannabis - on a massive scale.

Much ancient art might have been executed by cannabis users. Early Christian Popes condemned cannabis - perhaps because of links with pagan rituals.

Pictish cannabis pipes might still have been used in Scotland during the Middle Ages. Merchants in medieval St Andrews - a major centre for pilgrims - grew hemp in their gardens. This might have been for clothes or ropes. Equally, with pilgrims seeking "mystical" and "religious" experiences, merchants might have dealt in mind-affecting drugs. St Andrews had links with cannabis-using zones such as the Mediterranean.

Ancient Greek historians recorded widespread cannabis use by the Scythians - who lived around the Balkans and the Black Sea. The Scythians - held by some to have emigrated to Scotland to form the basis of Pictish society - were one of the few ethnic groups undefeated by Alexander the Great. Supporters of cannabis usage laud this as "proof" that acceptance of cannabis in a society renders that society strong and independent. Opponents of cannabis use would argue that the Scythian example suggests people who heavily use cannabis are highly aggressive.

As modern nation states emerged, rulers encouraged hemp-growing - to provide ropes and sails for navies. "Canvas" and "canvass" (meaning to sift) derive from the Old French word "canevas". "Canevas" translates as "cannabis". In Elizabethan England, it was for a time a criminal offence for farmers *not* to grow some hemp on their holdings. Some historians claim that Napoleon even invaded Russia - in the 18th century the world's largest hemp producer - in order to cut off hemp supplies to his enemies, who needed the plant's fibres to maintain their navies.

In various forms - especially tinctures - cannabis was on sale in Scotland until the early 20th century. Along with opium products such as laudanum (a tincture of opium), such products deadened pain, treated florid symptoms of mental illness and calmed children. It is not clear from the historical record that crime was associated with widespread use of cannabis - which might seem to support late-20th arguments for decriminalising the drug. But children frequently died from such ministrations.

In the United States, large commercial companies sold cannabis products. One such firm rejoiced in the title "Gangah Wallah Hasheesh Candy Company". The original Coca Cola contained cocaine.

As Scotland industrialised, drugs were both widely used and increasingly condemned. Workers used opiates to alleviate symptoms of respiratory diseases. The burgeoning 19th-century temperance movement actually promoted use of cannabis and laudanum as alternatives to alcohol.

In the 18th century, most opium was not imported, but was grown in North Norfolk and Cambridgeshire poppy fields. Use of opiates as anaesthetics was known in medieval Scotland. Quantities of such drugs were recovered during excavations at the medieval hospital site at Soutra Hill, south of Edinburgh. Before 20th-century cures emerged for serious illnesses, medical science could only offer opium-related palliatives.

Until the late-19th century, newspapers ran ads for quack remedies which contained opiates, cannabis or alcohol - or all three. "Dr Bateman's Pectoral Drops" claimed to cure "fluxes, spitting of blood, consumptions, agues, small-pox, measles, colds and coughs". Other "medicines" included "Dr Walker's Patent Jesuit Drops" - aimed at people with sexually transmitted diseases. Ads for "Lancaster Black Drop" were common - and emphasised that opiate's quality control.

Writer and journalist Thomas De Quincey, who lived in Glasgow in the mid-19th century, used opium. He called the drug "a panacea for all human woes".

De Quincey knew what late-20th century addicts know. Narcotics offer temporary mental oblivion to troubled people - but removal of drugs causes massive physical symptoms including violent stomach cramps, vomiting and pain. To counter these effects, addicts take even greater quantities of drugs. The ultimate in vicious circles results.

Apart from generalised accounts of opiates and cannabis usage among industrial workers - and occasional insights into tortured individuals such as De Quincey - serious public consideration of recognisably modern drugs issues does not appear until WW1. Mass casualties led to massive use of opiates-based pain killers. Hard-pressed doctors, nurses and ancillary staff on the Western Front began to use opiates to relieve feelings of helplessness, anger and alienation.

Many combatants on both sides during WW1 relied on stimulants such as benzedrines - "speed". Hermann Goering - a notorious user of morphine - claimed his addiction began with pain killers after being shot in the groin.

First significant anti-drugs legislation appeared in 1920. In 1922, in the first case of its kind in Scotland, a Glasgow pharmacist was convicted of supplying morphine sulphate to a man not authorised to possess it. The pharmacist had not recorded the name of the true recipient or purchaser, and falsely entered the name of a doctor. An addict had supplied others with the drug sold by the pharmacist.

On 1 June, 1922, *The Herald* reported:

"Charlotte Young (54), a woman of respectable appearance, was remitted to the sheriff

from the Central Police Court, Glasgow, yesterday, on a charge of having between 5 October, 1921, and 27 April last, obtained a number of tubes of morphine sulphate by uttering to a chemist prescriptions on which the signatures of medical practitioners had been forged. It is alleged that the woman, who was arrested in Aberdeen, received in all 132 tubes of morphine sulphate."

On 25 August, 1922, *The Herald* recorded:

"An Airdrie woman was charged with having obtained quantities of morphine sulphate from chemists by means of forged prescriptions. It was stated that on the prescriptions names were signed purporting to be the names of doctors. Quantities of the drug obtained at various times amounted in all to about 300 tubes."

Such post-WW1 reporting has a curiously modern tone:

"An agent for the accused stated that she was in ill health, had suffered from malaria, and it was for that reason that she first used the drug."

Such assertions might have been sophistry - designed to conceal organised crime's growing involvement in the drugs business.

Stimulants such as benzedrine are appetite suppressants - and drugs issued on Western Front battlefields became "slimming pills" on Civvy Street. These were not classified as poisons until 1934.

Cannabis was legally outlawed in 1928. In 1930, Glasgow detectives disguised as Indian pedlars arrested the "widow of a coloured man and proprietor of a cafe at Anderston Quay" for "harbouring immoral women and allowing men to smoke hashish". There were seizures of cannabis - invariably referred to as "Indian hemp" - at other Scottish ports such as Greenock and Dundee. In 1932, a cache of drugs, including cocaine, was found in a wood at Anniesland, Glasgow.

During WW2, newspapers carried short accounts of drugs cases, mostly in Glasgow - a major centre for US forces gathering for the invasion of mainland Europe. By the late-1950s, chief constables' reports began to highlight cases involving possession of "Indian hemp".

In 1960, there were 15 cases of illegal possession of barbituates in Glasgow. By 1963, such cases totalled 34. In 1964, 22 persons were convicted of possessing *cannabis* - "Indian hemp" was becoming a redundant term. In 1966, 57 persons were convicted in Glasgow on drugs charges. Terms such as "purple hearts" and "pep pills" appeared in media reports. Frequently, such offences were linked with forged prescriptions. By the 1950s, press reports told of increasing break-ins to doctors' cars and hospitals.

In 1971, reports in *The Herald* graphically showed the ease with which drugs users obtained quantities of morphine from "cooking" widely available proprietary medicines. Manufacturers have removed or drastically reduced such ingredients. But in 1997, a middle-aged Alloa housewife was convicted of breach of the peace, after inducing members of the public to purchase on her behalf large quantities of the cough medicine Actifed. She had been banned from pharmacies after becoming addicted to the stimulant pseudoephedrine - a constituent of the medicine.

A former nurse admitted addiction to Gee's Linctus and Benylin (containing tincture of opium):

"I've spent almost £2000 in the last two and a half years on Benylin. But now only six pharmacies in Scotland will sell to me. I've done a 500-mile trip to buy two bottles. My car had 12,500 miles on it three years ago. Now it's done 109,000 miles. Very little of that has been with passengers."

Societies such as Communist China and Cuba literally execute users and sellers. Societies such as Holland attempt to decriminalise and "tolerate". Other societies cope by "denial" - an approach which has in recent times operated in the West of Scotland. Until at least the mid-1980s, social workers in Strathclyde were forbidden, on pain of instant dismissal, to mention drugs problems affecting individuals in official reports to children's hearings and courts. Councillors apparently felt such references could affect Glasgow's growing image of social and economic regeneration.

In Strathclyde, police operate multi-faceted approaches to a complex and multi-faceted problem. In close liaison with other enforcement agencies such as HM Customs and Excise, every attempt is made to halt importation of drugs. Dealers are regularly "busted". Addicts are referred to helping agencies. And since the 1980s, police have been involved in anti-drugs education.

There is sometimes bitter debate about law enforcement, too. It can take HM Customs and Excise up to 24 hours to search *one* container of imported cargo. It would be impossible to search the many thousands of containers brought into the UK every day.

Such problems have led to so-called "intelligence-gathering" approaches to drugs importation - a process involving foreign governments, drugs agencies and police forces. In the late 1990s, it was proposed that, with the end of the Cold War, intelligence agencies should become involved in the planet's "war against drugs". Such approaches are necessarily covert - and customs services in particular have been attacked by some press, politicians, public opinion and trade unions who want anti-drugs measures, as with justice in general, "to be seen to be done".

In the past, most illegal drugs used in the UK were imported. In the late-20th century, there are disturbing signs that drugs are being grown or manufactured within the British Isles - as they were in the 18th century.

In Strathclyde, amphetamine "factories" have been uncovered in Dunbartonshire, Ayrshire and Lanarkshire. Cannabis plants are grown via hydroponics - in which plants are nurtured in water containing nutrient salts.

One man produced between 40 and 60 kilos of cannabis per year for five years. This could have earned him up to £80,000 per annum - much of which he invested in legitimate businesses such as property development. Police officers point out that this does not represent harmless dissidents simply growing the plant for their own use. Hydroponic equipment is extremely expensive - and such cases reveal highly capitalised commercial businesses.

At the end of the 20th century, many users of heroin in Strathclyde appear to have moved from injecting the drug into smoking it - "chasing the dragon". Some users believe that smoking heroin is less addictive than injecting it. It is estimated that there are in the late-1990s perhaps 7,000 people in Glasgow addicted to heroin. A few years earlier, this might have been as high as 10,000.

If there has been a reduction in addict numbers, this might be a reflection of the region's continued use of "multi-agency" approaches to drugs problems - in which police work closely with social workers, housing providers, medical services and education authorities.

Some police officers, along with sections of political opinion and the media, favour decriminalisation of drugs such as cannabis. Other opinion is equally determined that such moves would effectively constitute surrender to perhaps the worst social evil to affect late-20th century society. ☐

ON A PLATE

L AW enforcement in the West of Scotland has always had to deal with the activities of counterfeiters. In 1751, forged halfpennies - "coined at Birmingham of a very base metal" - circulated in Glasgow. The authorities feared dud coins might turn up in church collection plates. In the 18th and early 19th centuries, Scottish banks needed to instill public confidence in then new-fangled paper money. Accordingly, they honoured forged notes!

In 1789, Neil McLean forged guinea notes of the Glasgow Arms Bank and was sentenced to death. Counterfeit halfpennies also circulated - "to the detriment of the lieges".

In 1800, Glasgow's Thistle Bank offered £100 reward for information on forgers copying its five-shilling notes. Forgers seldom produced notes of such large denominations as to attract attention and comment. Pound notes were ideal and were readily passed at markets and fairs. School teachers, discharged soldiers and French PoWs were among those who dabbled in forgery in 18th-century Scotland. The Crown Office left prosecution of forgers to the banks themselves.

Sometimes, culprits were executed. At other times, clemency was exercised - and forgers were transported to the colonies as indentured servants, usually to the Caribbean.

In 1844, "coiners" were caught in a house in Glasgow's Old Vennel, with £1 worth of coins in their possession - "all base but shining bright, and apparently just new from the moulds". In 1851, a house in Glasgow's Marlborough Street contained crucibles and moulds for casting pennies, along with "all the apparatus for coining on a large scale". Counterfeit pennies sold at 30/- worth for £1 to hawkers. Small traders "got rid of them in retail transactions with the lower orders".

In January 1848, *The Herald* reported apprehension of a "gang of coiners" in Coatbridge:

"The police, under the direction of Inspector Walker, immediately after capturing the coining party, set out in search of the mint, and were fortunate enough to seize their whole apparatus together with the material for making as many coins as would keep Coatbridge supplied for a long time to come. The party consisted of Marriot Hay, his wife, his son, and a lodger, who carried on business at Pottery Row on the banks of the Monkland Canal, a little above Coatbridge."

Victorian Glasgow's best known forger was John Henry Greatrex - "a tall, good looking man, and an impressive preacher". A regular speaker on Glasgow Green, Greatrex's flowing beard gave him the appearance of an Old Testament prophet.

Greatrex was a professional photographer - with a fashionable studio in town. To impress customers with his piety, he hung Biblical texts around his studio. His assistant was a young woman called Jane Weir. Jane - usually known as Jenny - was also his paramour. Greatrex soon tired of photographing douce Glaswegians, however. He turned to capturing images of £1 notes issued by the Union Bank of Scotland. Results were poor - and Greatrex sought help from Sewell Grimshaw, an expert copper engraver.

Sewell's brother Tom provided necessary capital, and in early 1866 a lease was taken on a new photographic studio in Sauchiehall Street. Little photography was done there, but by the summer of 1866 the trio had printed more than 1300 Union Bank notes. These were passed in Glasgow and surrounding towns, and as far afield as Aberdeen. Greatrex and Jenny were in Aberdeen when they learned of the arrest of the Grimshaw brothers.

The pair fled to America, travelling via Southampton and sailing to New York on separate ships. Superintendent Alexander McCall, chief of Glasgow's detective force, tracked them to New York. There, reckoning Greatrex and Weir might be low on funds, he advertised in the city's newspapers, offering employment in a photographic studio for an experienced female assistant. Preference would be given to "a Scotch girl".

Jenny Weir applied for the job, writing from the boarding house where she was living with Greatrex. The couple were out when McCall went there, but the landlady recognised Jenny from the superintendent's description. Greatrex had shaved off his beard, but still quoted Scripture. When Greatrex and Weir returned to the house, they were arrested.

Greatrex and the Grimshaws were tried at the High Court at Edinburgh. Greatrex was sentenced to 20 years' imprisonment, while the Grimshaws each got 15 years.

Three years later, McCall became chief constable of Glasgow. Jane Weir's letter of application is in Strathclyde Police Museum.

WW1 brought new opportunities for skilled forgers. In 1914, after tenants of a Glasgow flat emigrated, their landlord found in the basement equipment used to produce counterfeit half crowns.

As casualty lists mounted - Scotland lost 100,000 men of military age between 1914 and 1918 - many people bought from forgers fake certificates "confirming" holders had been discharged from the armed forces. Accounts of court cases involving forged discharge documents were frequently reported throughout WW1. Forged money continued to be passed throughout Strathclyde, too.

Growing use of illegal drugs such as morphine and cocaine were another consequence of WW1. Doctors, nurses and other hospital workers had ample opportunities to acquire addictions, while serving in field hospitals on the Western Front. Many wounded soldiers who were given large and repeated doses of narcotics and pain killers also became addicts. Post-WW1, newspapers increasingly carried stories about drugs - and highlighted the role of forgers. Prescriptions were being forged as early as 1922.

Forged money continued to circulate widely during the inter-war years. In 1932, George Dickson, resident in a Glasgow model lodging house since release from prison in 1923, was sentenced to three years' penal servitude for possessing a mould for producing counterfeit sixpences. Dickson was known in the city as "The Coiner".

WW2 provided further opportunities for skilled forgers. Soon after rationing was introduced, thousands of Clydesiders claimed they'd "lost" their ration books. Forged ration coupons were used to purchase food, clothing and furniture.

In 1947, an inhabitant of another Glasgow "model" was arrested for being drunk and incapable. Police officers discovered he was carrying three counterfeit Bank of Scotland £1 notes. A search at the lodging house uncovered an extraordinary counterfeiting kit.

The "plates" were engraved by hand on roofing slate. A court dealt leniently with the forger, who possessed considerable artistic ability. He received nine months' imprisonment. Police officers seem to have recognised this man wasn't a "serious" forger - and apparently helped him find a job. But in 1951, he was arrested on another charge of forgery. One of his plates is displayed in Strathclyde Police Museum.

Some rationing endured until the mid-1950s, along with occasional cases of coupon-forging.

In the 1980s, reviewing the impact of the welfare state on Clydeside, the sociological weekly *New Society* suggested that introduction of social security benefits such as Family Allowance had assisted criminal activity by allowing benefit books to be "signed over" to illegal moneylenders. In similar vein, there were cases of such books being forged - with at least one suggestion that the proceeds of such activity might have helped finance terrorist groups in Northern Ireland.

Post-war advances in reprographic technology, such as the introduction of photocopiers and offset litho printing, allowed increasingly sophisticated forgery.□

FAGIN ON BROOMIELAW

THE birch and birching table displayed in Strathclyde Police Museum are grim reminders that law enforcement has always been closely involved with juveniles in the West of Scotland.

In the early 19th century, no distinction was made between adult and juvenile offenders. In 1830, a boy - "about ten years of age" - was sent to the Glasgow Bridewell for 60 days for stealing two books from a shop. In 1851, Donald MacDonald, aged 10, was sentenced to 20 days in Inveraray Jail for stealing 12lbs of cheese from a shop in Dunoon.

From 1854, children who committed petty crimes were sentenced to short spells in prison, followed by several years in reformatory schools, or, from 1866, industrial schools.

In 1856, Margaret Cowan, aged 11, from Bowmore, Islay, was sentenced to 14 days imprisonment at Inverary, followed by three years in a Glasgow reformatory. Shortage of reformatories meant children were often placed far from their homes. A century later, similar problems led to "the wee boarded out boys" who lived with crofters' families in the Highlands and Islands. Many were physically or sexually abused.

Cases of absconding at Glasgow's Parkhead Reformatory for Boys were "very numerous". In Glasgow in 1897, "eleven-year-old incorrigible James Montgomery" went to a reformatory for five years - for stealing 2/- and treating his friends to coffee and cookies.

Children could be transported. In 1836, in Glasgow, William Waugh, a little boy "by habit and repute a thief", was convicted of housebreaking and transported for seven years. The same sentence was imposed on another small Glasgow boy, John Murphy. He sighed in the dock and said: "It'll wear awa."

But early police forces in Strathclyde also had as part of their duties protection of vulnerable children. In 1816, *The Herald* reported:

"Wednesday forenoon, a girl of six years of age was enticed from her father's door, Glen Street, Paisley, by a woman who pretended to send her on an errand. She took the girl into a close and robbed her of her earrings. Diligent search was made for the woman and she was taken to the police office. Her name is Jean Mulloch, of Gorbals of Glasgow."

Many children were cruelly exploited by parents or guardians. In Glasgow in 1833, nine-year-old James McEwan stole a tankard from a pub. A court was told:

"His stepmother is a worthless character, who daily sends him to the streets to beg. He has been found at least 10 times at midnight, starving with cold and hunger."

In one week of February 1839, Glasgow's Night Asylum for the Houseless temporarily sheltered 631 people - including 124 boys and 118 girls. That year, police in Glasgow found three destitute children - the youngest about four - wandering the streets "in the most abject wretchedness and poverty". Also in 1839, Glasgow's new House of Refuge for juveniles admitted more than 200 boys "wandering in rags about the streets by day, sleeping on cold stairs by night".

Throughout the 19th century, desperate women abandoned their children. In 1848, *The Herald* reported:

"A stout fresh-complexioned young woman called at the house of Elizabeth Colquhoun, Kirk Street, Calton, Glasgow, and requested to rest there for the night, which was allowed her, although she was unknown to the inmates, and it is not a lodging house. Shortly afterwards, she went out, stating she would be back in a few minutes. She left a male child apparently a few weeks old, and no clue has been discovered as to her whereabouts."

In January 1849, *The Herald* reported:

"A woman named Neill, residing near the Broomielaw, was charged with harbouring vagrant children, and encouraging them in evil practices. This woman had been keeping several boys in her house, whose occupation is to prowl the streets of the harbour, and beg or steal whatever they can lay their hands on. The plunder is disposed of by the mistress of the house, who retains one half of the proceeds for her trouble, and by this means is enabled to indulge her favourite propensity for whisky.

"She was sent to the Bridewell for 60 days and the boys were transferred to the industrial or ragged school. Our readers may regret the existence of such a state of affairs in our city, but we assure them this is no solitary or unusual instance. There are many such nurseries for crime in Glasgow, fostered by the pernicious practice of giving alms to street beggars, and they are allowed to multiply by the apathy and neglect which seems to pervade the better classes in regard to the moral and spiritual condition of the masses who inhabit the more wretched localities of our city.

"Those best acquainted with the matter state that until public feeling is aroused to the necessity of rescuing the young savages who abound in our wynds and closes from the moral darkness in which they are enveloped, there will be little improvement in the social conditions of those wretched inhabitants of our city, and the prisons will always be full."

Glasgow's Ragged School was designed to accommodate hundreds of destitute children, described as "the arabs of the city". Many slipped through such safety nets. In 1855, eight-year-old Thomas Gardner or Garvan - already well known to the police as "a rogue and vagabond" - tried to pick ladies' pockets at Glasgow's Broomielaw steamboat wharf. His sentence was 60 days' imprisonment and five years in a reformatory school.

Abandoned or detained children were the lucky ones in 19th-century Strathclyde. In 1873, *The Herald* reported:

"James Monteith, flint miller, residing at Maryhill, Glasgow, while engaged in clearing

the mill-race at the lower Garrioch mills, observed a bundle in the water, which he took out and found to contain the body of a male child, wrapped in a piece of old cotton cloth, with a piece of twine round its neck and a stone attached."

By the late-19th century, the role played by destitution in juvenile crime was recognised by some far-sighted people and efforts were made to provide occupations and shelters for homeless young people. In 1866, the sum of £40 was raised to equip the Bath Street premises of the Glasgow Shoe Black Brigade with 12 beds for homeless boys.

In WW1 tens of thousands of fathers, who traditionally wielded a heavy hand in Scottish homes, left for the trenches. Mothers worked in war industries. In 1917, 11-year-old James Kelter stole a pocket book containing five 10/- notes. He was sent to the training ship Mars for five years. His downfall was attributed to "the lure of the ice-cream shop coupled with the attraction of the picture-house".

Also in 1917, another 11-year-old Glasgow boy, Samuel Levy, received six strokes of the birch for assaulting a girl with a knife. In 1918, 13-year-old William McGregor stole provisions from a Glasgow shop - and went to the training ship Empress for three years.

Magistrates could order birching of any boy more than eight years of age. A birch rod consisted of a bundle of dry twigs bound together. Girls were exempt from such punishment.

In 1897, nine-year-old James Mackay stole 1/- from a Glasgow shop, and received seven strokes of the birch. In 1913 alone, courts in Scotland ordered 407 boys to be birched. During WW1, there was a remarkable increase in use of the birch. Eight hundred boys were birched in 1916, 925 in 1917, and 755 in 1918.

Reforming pressures continued, too. In 1926, Ayrshire-based anarchist and ecologist Dugald Semple issued a surprisingly modern-sounding challenge to penally orientated thinking on juvenile issues:

"One of the greatest evils of life in cities is that children are growing up with no love of nature."

By 1928, the number of birchings fell to 135. But by 1936, the number of boys birched in Scotland had risen to 230 - 69 of them in Glasgow. As late as 1943, questions were asked in the House of Commons after Renfrewshire's chief constable said he would use the "green birch" on young offenders and "cut them with it".

WW2 evacuation uprooted thousands of urban children from their homes and familiar surroundings. As in 1914-18, fathers joined the services, while mothers worked in factories and munitions plants. Shortly before the outbreak of war, Glasgow's chief constable, Percy Sillitoe, reported a gratifying decrease in juvenile crime. By 1940, he was suggesting that lighting restrictions and closed schools might lead to a "war-time juvenile crime wave".

Reporting on child neglect during 1940, the Glasgow committee of the Royal Scottish Society for the Prevention of Cruelty to Children expressed concern about the number of mothers alleged to have lost interest in their homes and children. Lack of companionship and absence of husbands on military service were given as reasons for the problem.

In 1941, Sillitoe described the increase in juvenile delinquency as "alarming" - and blamed part-time schooling for the problem. A 15-year-old Glasgow boy was sent to an approved school after being convicted of grabbing bundles of banknotes from five city banks. He spent the money "on amusements and gambling schools". Also in 1941, two Clydeside youths received borstal terms for looting articles from a bombed ARP depot.

In 1943, three boys - two aged 14 and one aged 15 - appeared at Glasgow Sheriff Juvenile Court charged with stealing 12 motor cars, two taxis, a motor van and a naval lorry from streets in the city centre. Five Glasgow boys took part in "bombing escapades" after stealing hand grenades from a Home Guard depot.

Also in 1943, four boys - two aged six - wrecked Renfrew County Library in Paisley. They smashed light fittings, damaged thousands of books and scattered 30,000 index cards. That year, a Glasgow child guidance clinic reported:

"Children are finding the departure of their fathers on war service a much more shattering experience than bombs falling outside their front doors".

A Glasgow newspaper blamed juvenile delinquency on "gadabout mothers". In 1945, three Glasgow youths, living rough in an air raid shelter, broke into offices and warehouses. They were sentenced to three years in borstal.

The post-WW2 decades saw intensification of the "care v control" debate in relation to juvenile offenders. A Glasgow Corporation report on war-time delinquency revealed that 2% of the city's children had appeared in court during the war - and blamed lax parenting, working mothers, and over-exposure to cinema.

Last birching was inflicted in 1948 - the year of full introduction of welfare state principles. Detention centres were set up for offenders between 14 and 21 as an alternative to approved schools and borstals.

The issue of birching died away until the "rediscovery" of juvenile offending in the 1960s - when there were renewed calls for its reintroduction. In 1966, an Ayrshire minister wrote to *The Herald:*

"I think any right-minded person, myself included, would be willing to administer the birch. Someone said at the Assembly that British police would not be willing to administer the birch. If the police did object, I myself would certainly birch a person convicted of a crime of violence."

In juvenile courts, sheriffs were replaced with lay persons - and in the early 1970s, courts were replaced with children's hearings. These were intended as "problem-solving" institutions - involving the community with children and families, via volunteer members drawn from regional "panels".

There are still claims that children's hearings are "soft" on offending - along with calls for restoration of fines on parents. But politicians generally have supported the system - which remains unique to Scotland, despite considerable attention from many other countries.

Police officers in Strathclyde continue to operate "twin track" approaches to juveniles. Co-operating with social workers, doctors and teachers, police officers - particularly via specialist female and child units - deal with offences against children. In the late-20th century, greater awareness of child abuse - sexual, physical and emotional - has resulted in many successful prosecutions of paedophiles and other offenders against children.

At the same time, officers deal with offending by children. The pendulum of public opinion swings constantly on that - and police officers have always operated within such inconsistencies. In the 1930s, Percy Sillitoe used force to deal with gang warfare in Glasgow. He also understood why many young people became offenders - and identified unemployment and deprivation as causes of crime.

In the late-20th century, police officers - as part of their community involvement role and as volunteer citizens - help ensure children obtain Dugald Semple's wish that they become closer to nature. Sillitoe and Semple would be delighted to hear that - and to know that the birch remains firmly retained in a glass case for posterity.□

THE GENTLE SEX?

FROM images of alleged murderer Madeleine Smith, through insights into the activities of forger's accomplice Jenny Weir, and a policewoman's uniform from the 1940s, Strathclyde Police Museum is a reminder that crime has always been something of an "equal opportunity employer".

In medieval times, punishments for women offenders involved public humiliation and physical discomfort. In 1584, Janet Foirside was found guilty of "sclander", and magistrates ordered "the brankis to be put in her mowth".

In 1588, Glasgow's kirk session ordered "ane commoun cart" in which to parade harlots before they were "doukit in Clyde". In 1599, troubled by "monifauld blasphemis and evill wordis usit be sundrie wemen", Glasgow constructed "ane pair joges". As late as the 17th century, "talkative drunken wives" were soused in the "cock stool" or ducking stool.

But, until comparatively recent times, most women offenders were convicted of theft

or prostitution - and sometimes both. In 1780, a grazier crossing Glasgow Bridge was accosted by "a girl of the town". She "artfully picked his pocket" of a watch and some money.

In 1793, Mary Douglas, guilty of housebreaking in Bridgeton, was whipped through the streets of Glasgow, and banished from Scotland for life.

From Glasgow's "correction house", women were shipped to plantations in Virginia. Cash paid to merchants for their transportation was no more than £1 per head. Real profits came from selling women to planters in America.

By 1839, an observer described women in one of Glasgow's common lodging houses:

"Ten, twelve and sometimes twenty persons, of both sexes and all ages, sleep promiscuously on the floor, in different degrees of nakedness. Many of the younger girls, and there are a multitude of them who frequent these places, appear to have been driven there from sheer want, and apply to the head of police to be rescued from misery, in great numbers. No efficient aid can be afforded them under existing institutions, and hundreds in a year become inured to crime, and pass through a rapid career of prostitution, drunkenness, and disease, to an early grave."

In 1844, a Glasgow woman named Violet Dailly appeared in court "gaily dressed" - and was sentenced to 60 days for brothel-keeping. In 1855, a gentleman was "decoyed" into a brothel in Gallowgate, Glasgow, and robbed of his gold watch, coat, boots and umbrella.

In 1836, between 30 and 40 "abandoned females" were charged with being "street pests" in and around Glasgow's High Street.

In 1850, police raided a brothel in Trongate, Glasgow, and arrested "two showily dressed females named Louisa Fitzcharles and Ann Wilson". They were each fined £5 - which they "paid readily". Most were less fortunate. In 1862, a prostitute called Helen Campbell was found dead from drink and exposure "in a sitting position, leaning against a wall" in Glasgow's Oswald Street.

In 1869, *The Herald* noted efforts in Glasgow on behalf of prostitutes:

"Dalbeth Institute for Penitent Women - the appeal on behalf of this institution, conducted by the Ladies of the Good Shepherd, appears in our advertising columns today."

The ad stated:

"The Aid of the Charitable is earnestly invoked on behalf of the Institution. Founded 18 years ago, the House has been enlarged so as to accommodate 150. There are 72 at present harboured in it, and the Reformatory School, in connection with the same House, contains 100 girls."

Throughout the 19th century, a stream of women and girls passed through courts in the West of Scotland, charged with theft. In 1805, Jean Craig, "alias Widow Marsden", stole cotton yarn from a cart in Glasgow's Bridgegate. She was sentenced to six months' imprisonment, and banished from Glasgow for life. In 1820, three Glasgow girls, "who for some time had partly lived by public charity and partly by gathering bones", were convicted of theft and banished for seven years. Women with previous convictions faced transportation.

In 1826, "known thief" Jean Livingston was transported to a penal colony for seven years for filching a pocket book containing £15 from Neil Walker in a Glasgow tavern.

Market days brought country people into Strathclyde towns, offering pickings for thieves of both sexes. The problem featured in popular song:

> *"I cam tae Glesca toon ae nicht*
> *Tae spend ma penny fee*
> *A bonny young lass she gied consent tae bear me company."*

In 1833, in a restaurant in Bell Street, Glasgow, two girls engaged a farmer in conversation and relieved him of a valuable silver watch. One was described as:

"a most experienced thief, particularly on market days, among the gash folk from the country".

In 1839, Gorbals police arrested a gang of female housebreakers. In 1844, Mary Boyle - "in appearance a gentle and interesting girl about 16 years of age" - was sentenced in Glasgow to transportation for 10 years for housebreaking.

In 1836, Anne Spalding got 60 days for stealing horsehair stuffing from the seats of Glasgow hackney cabs. Also in 1836, a Glasgow woman was charged with stealing a 56lb weight from a plumber's shop. She claimed it had been "thrown into her lap" by another woman as she innocently passed along a street.

In 1815, Elizabeth Greenhorn, a collier, was accused of murdering her baby, whose body had been found in the Old Monkland pit, near Glasgow. A court heard:

"She absented herself from work about twelve o'clock that day, under pretence of having a headache, and was afterwards found wandering in the pit, almost in a state of insensibility, and having every appearance of recent delivery.

"Greenhorn was convicted of concealing her pregnancy and was sentenced to one month's imprisonment."

"Child-stripping" was a common crime in early Victorian times and was referred to by Charles Dickens in *Dombey and Son*. Middle-class children, wearing expensive clothes and shoes, were favourite targets. In 1830, "a respectable young girl" was enticed into a close in Glasgow's Stockwell Street and stripped of her shoes. Such robberies were reported to be "of frequent occurrence". Child-strippers were frequently female. In 1836, a four-year-old boy was abducted from Adelphi Street, Gorbals, "by one of those abandoned females who go about stripping children of their clothes". Stolen clothing ended up in "wee pawns" in the city's Trongate.

Victorian criminology reflected the "madonna/whore" syndrome. A "naturally" good woman was "the angel in the house". A criminal woman was "the worst of all creations". Female criminals faced harsher condemnation than their male counterparts. They were ostracised by respectable society. Ironically, exclusion made it difficult for them to reform. In the Victorian era, one in four Scottish women were domestic servants. A conviction for theft or prostitution denied access to that job market - and such jobs also provided food and shelter.

In Georgian and Victorian times, when spirits were much stronger than their modern equivalents, alcohol was a frequent contributory factor in female offending. Crimes such as pocket-picking in taverns were committed by tipsy women to raise more money for alcohol.

Similarly, many prostitutes fed their alcohol addictions. By the late-19th century, women were refused access to most Scottish pubs, but drink could still be obtained from licensed grocers and unlicensed shebeens, and considerable numbers of women were arrested on charges of breach of the peace and being drunk and disorderly.

In 1899, Glasgow Corporation purchased the mansion of Girgenti, Ayrshire, and equipped it as a reformatory for "degraded drunken women". Girgenti was 21 miles from Glasgow, stood in extensive grounds, and accommodated 50 women. They were to be reformed by:

"immunity from all bibulous temptation, pure air, and horticultural work of a light nature".

Experiments with anti-alcohol drugs proved a failure. Not surprisingly, many inmates absconded.

Girgenti was judged:

"insufficient for the segregation of all the worst of the Glasgow drunken women".

Undeterred, Glasgow Corporation seriously considered banishing drunkards of both sexes to the island of Shuna, Argyll. Councillors even obtained a quotation for shipping people to Shuna. In the 1930s, there were suggestions that Glasgow's alcohol abusers should be exiled to St Kilda.

Other influences - including leading police officers - placed alcohol and prostitution in a wider context. In 1908, Glasgow's chief constable complained that the law was insufficiently strong to deal with pimps. The law allowed a maximum punishment of three months' imprisonment for living off immoral earnings. There were also moves to appoint female workers - precursors of female police officers - to tackle such issues within a policing context.

In 1909, *The Herald* reported:

"In Los Angeles, Miss Fanny Bixby, daughter of a Californian millionaire, has been appointed as a 'policeman' by the Long Beach municipal authority. She will carry out social work among women under official auspices - mainly involving seeking out and trying to reform wayward and fallen girls."

Female bookies also appeared in Strathclyde. In 1917, Mary Ventry was arrested in Glasgow with 45 betting slips and £7 in her possession. In 1937, Agnes Mitchell - aka "Aggie the Bookie" - was charged with offering a 10/- bribe to a police officer in a close in Glasgow's Scotia Street. She was alleged to have said: "Here ye are. Now keep away."

Fortune telling - illustrated by the crystal ball in Strathclyde Police Museum - led to many women appearing in court during the inter-war years. In 1922, a Glasgow fortune teller told an undercover policewoman:

"You will marry a tall, dark man and live to a good old age."

A few minutes later, she gave an identical reading to another customer - who also happened to be an undercover cop.

But by 1912, Glasgow's chief constable pointed out that women convicted of importuning simply paid fines and continued their lifestyle. That year, 132 brothel-keepers were convicted in the city.

By 1913, it was claimed that foyers of increasingly luxurious cinemas were "patrolled" by prostitutes. Jessie and William Mackay were convicted of running a disorderly house at 189 Pitt Street, Glasgow. They were said to have earned up to £1000 a year. Young women observed entering the house were described as "better-class girls engaged in some occupation or in keeping house for respectable parents".

William Mackay claimed well-known male citizens prevailed on him to allow them to bring women to his premises. He used the telephone to summon women to his large flat. One girl admitted earning up to £20 a week - half of which went to the Mackays.

There were suggestions that the Mackays might have been pressed into brothel-keeping to repay debts - and the couple claimed they were being blackmailed by "powerful people". The world of 189 Pitt Street was a long way from drunken taverns in the city's East End - organised crime involving women was emerging. In 1924, a brothel in the West End of Glasgow was described as "rivalling a nightclub in opulence".

Abortions, illegal until 1967, led to numerous court appearances by women. In 1933, "two well-dressed women" were jailed in Glasgow for performing an abortion on a girl of 18. Two other women were charged with running a house in which married women could give birth to children, and then give them up for adoption by registering the births as if they had taken place to single women.

WW2 brought an increase in prostitution. In 1943, a fiscal asked for jail sentences without fine options for five Glasgow women convicted of soliciting:

"The women parade about the street, neither working nor wanting. That isn't right at all when there is plenty of useful employment for them."

Despite such problems, Scotland was slow to appoint policewomen. Although by 1916 there were more than 2000 "women patrols" in the UK, they were used in most cities to visit cinemas and "report on the nature of the entertainment provided". They also assisted male officers "in the parks". *The Herald* opined:

"It is doubtful, however, whether many women will give up their whole time to this public service."

But women had served in the forces, and replaced men in industry. And they were moving - full-time - into aspects of policing. In 1917, *The Herald* reported:

"Among many important parts of the machinery that will win the war the Women Police take a place. They are given work of responsibility and trust. Conditions of service are good - 25/- a week towards expenses during three weeks' training and 47/6d a week on appointment. Police Women provide their own uniform. Patriotic and educated women are required to enrol into the Women Police Force of Munitions Factories."

Outwith munitions factories, pay for "women patrols" was much lower.

Even after WW1, women police officers were thin on the ground. In 1919, Scotland's royal burghs were asked if they were in favour of policewomen. All but seven curtly dismissed the idea. The 1920 Committee on the Employment of Women on Police Duties - the Baird Committee - heard that only 13 women had been appointed as "police auxiliaries" in Scotland - 10 in Glasgow, two in Edinburgh and one in Ayr. England had 400 such "auxiliaries". The official view was:

"Women could not possibly be paid the same as men since they would not be taking the same risks".

Scotland's county councils told the Baird Committee their forces did not need or want women officers. HM Inspector of Constabulary admitted that though 10 "auxiliaries" had been theoretically appointed in Glasgow, only three had actually taken up post - "as an experiment". The City of Glasgow Police had a woman - Miss Emily Miller - who took statements from women and girls, mostly victims of sex crimes. Miss Miller told the Baird Committee she personally rarely came into contact with offenders, but she wanted women officers with powers of arrest. Glasgow's chief constable grudgingly admitted that women officers could do some jobs, but claimed it was difficult to find the "right type". Miss Miller claimed that low pay - 35/- a week - was a major obstacle.

Miss Edith Tancred, director of the Scottish Training School for Policewomen, founded in 1918 in Glasgow's Newton Place, also gave evidence. Up to 1920, the school had trained Women's Royal Air Force patrols and an additional three women - two of whom worked for the National Vigilance Association in Edinburgh. Miss Tancred agreed with Miss Miller - poor pay, no powers of arrest and no pensions made police work unattractive to women. Ayr's policewoman didn't even have a room in which to conduct interviews with women and girls - and used her own bed-sitter.

Strongest opposition to policewomen came from the Scottish Police Federation. A spokesman said:

"It is not that the Scottish police are antagonistic to the employment of women, but any thinking man who knows anything about police work does not want to see a woman touching it all. It is not a thing for women."

Lieutenant Robert Sweeney of Glasgow City Police was more enlightened - although still patronising. He thought women officers should have the status of male officers, but only three-quarters the wage. Sweeney thought women would be particularly useful in watching cinemas, since up-market prostitutes used cinema lounges as "places of assignation". Sweeney admitted he'd seen a Glasgow tram conductress run after a thief and hold him until police arrived. But he still saw little future for women on the force:

"A man joins the police for a career, but a woman only joins until she gets a husband."

Women who married had to leave Scottish forces until 1968.

In the mid-1920s, a Scottish Office circular stated that women police should take statements relating to sexual offences. In 1927, the Scottish Police Federation agreed to represent female colleagues. In 1931, soon after appointment as Glasgow's chief constable, Percy Sillitoe increased the number of women in his force to 15 and raised their wages. By 1932, policewomen had to be unmarried, or widows, not under 22 or over 35. Minimum height was 5' 4".

Women's duties still concentrated on sexual offences involving women and children. In October, 1932, Percy Sillitoe appointed Janet Gray as a woman sergeant, at a wage of £5 a week. The increased number of women continued to patrol streets and parks and visited dance halls, cinemas and theatres. They were particularly effective in cases of fortune telling and shoplifting.

By 1935, there were 28 policewomen in Scotland - 15 of them in Glasgow, attached to the CID. The city had 2232 male officers. In his annual report, Sillitoe recorded:

"Experience has shown them to be invaluable in certain phases of police work, such as taking statements in sexual offences."

By 1940, Glasgow had 15 women officers, Ayr two, Motherwell and Wishaw two, Paisley two, Dumbarton one, Lanark six, and Renfrew one. At the beginning of WW2, Sillitoe extended his special constables' recruiting campaign to create a Women's Auxiliary Police Corps. Initially comprising 20 women, the WAPC took over many police duties. Most WAPC recruits drove vehicles and carried out canteen or telephone duties, but 14 auxiliaries accompanied regular women officers and were given powers of arrest. A number of WAPC members joined the City of Glasgow Police after 1945.

By the 1950s, women's police duties were growing considerably. On June 11, 1955, *The Herald* reported:

"After a man broke away from his police escort in Rutherglen Road, Glasgow, last night, several shots were fired in the direction of a policeman and policewoman who followed him. When she saw the man pursued by Constable Alexander Davidson, policewoman Isabella Rankine, of Lanarkshire Constabulary, who was at a bus stop, joined him. Several people spoke of the bravery of policewoman Rankine, who followed closely on the man's heels for several hundred yards."

By 1958, there were 74 policewomen in Glasgow, headed by a superintendent. The chief constable reported:

"During the year, seven policewomen were commended for their work in connection with the arrest of criminals on charges of theft by housebreaking, attempted theft by opening lockfast places and theft. Commendations were also issued to each of two other policewomen for intelligent and determined action at the scene of a gassing fatality."

In 1962, Superintendent Janet Gray became an Assistant Inspector of Constabulary for Scotland. The comparatively small number of policewomen in Scotland meant her appointment was on a part-time basis.
But in 1969, *The Herald* reported:

"Miss Margaret Lang, a 24-year-old Dumbarton policewoman, will next week become Britain's first woman beat bobby.
"She will take over four square miles of Dumbarton in the reorganisation of Dumbarton and the Vale of Leven to unit beat policing.
"A call from her beat will rally support from a group of a dozen men. She will work from her home in Bellsmyre housing scheme, the heart of her beat."

In the 1970s, along with "rediscovery" of poverty in society, it was increasingly acknowledged that abuse of children had reasserted itself also. In 1972, it was estimated that six in every 1000 live children born would be assaulted by their parents or guardians. At least 60% of them would be severely beaten - 10% would die, and 15% would suffer permanent brain damage. By the 1980s, such awareness grew to include the acceptance of previously "hidden" sexual abuse of young people. This perhaps refocussed the work of many women officers. In addition, more and more women proved willing to report offences such as rape, leading to the development of female and child units in many forces, including Strathclyde.

Helped by intensive media campaigns in the 1990s, domestic violence - which had attracted surprisingly severe responses from Victorian courts - became increasingly unacceptable. and women were more prepared to report assaults in the home to the police. All officers - male and female - were trained to regard domestic violence as a serious matter and to refer victims to specialist agencies such as Victim Support or Women's Aid.

Despite "unisex" staffing of female and child units, a "core" of women officers was retained should a female complainer wish to speak solely with a same-sex officer.

In 1945, there were approximately 50,000 regular policemen in the UK - and only 500 regular policewomen. In Strathclyde, in 1997, there were approximately 6000 constables - of whom 1000 were women. The force had one female chief superintendent and four female superintendents. With the advent of equal opportunities recruitment, training and staff development policies, indications were that female constables would gradually, as individually appropriate, "move up through the ranks". In 1998, a senior female officer described the 'revolution':

"Twenty years ago, a woman officer would have known the names of all her female colleagues."

As women played an increasing role in combatting crime, offences among women both altered and remained similar to 19th century patterns. Particularly in Glasgow, street prostitution continued - and a number of prostitutes met violent deaths during the 1990s. Strathclyde Police responded to these incidents by increasing surveillance in Glasgow city centre and by visiting the homes of men known to have been kerb-crawling at or near times when prostitutes were violently killed. These measures received considerable support from politicians, women's groups and the media.

Female offenders continued to play a substantial role in thefts from shops - often associated with drugs addiction and the acknowledged poverty in which many lone female parents live in the West of Scotland.

Although experienced officers observed that women offenders did not significantly take part in initial thefts of items such as cashcards or cheques, they did however play prominent roles in frauds involving such stolen items. Jenny Weir has her late-20th century counterparts.

In the heyday of allegedly prevalent gang warfare - the age of Clydeside's "razor kings" - women commonly concealed weapons for their male associates. In the 1990s, both women and men are routinely searched on entering discotheques, clubs and similar premises in urban Strathclyde. However, that "equal opportunities" scenario is not reflected in drugs issues - where, it seems, women are still prepared to "take the rap" by storing drugs on behalf of husbands, boyfriends and other male associates.

But in 1998, following the widely publicised drugs-related death of a 13-year-old Glasgow boy, newspapers reported that many such women had in fact "shopped" men for whom they had previously been willing or unwilling accomplices.

Despite considerable areas of similarity between male and female offenders, noticeable areas of divergence remain. Although as many women now hold driving licences as men, women commit considerably fewer traffic offences - and driving under the influence of drink remains very much a male offence.❑

"NO FINER SQUADS"

STRATHCLYDE Police Museum displays an officer wearing a steel helmet and carrying a gas mask. The museum also features medals won by officers during both WW1 and WW2.

Until 1914, wars had little effect on policing in Strathclyde. Wars were fought by professional soldiers. Territorial units didn't go into action until the Boer War.

In August 1914, along with tens of thousands of young men from communities throughout Strathclyde, police officers flocked to the colours.

Within a few months, more than 300 Glasgow officers had joined the Army or Navy. Most Glasgow officers who enlisted early in the war joined the elite Scots Guards.

Glasgow police officers were highly valued by the Army. In 1914, a senior Scots Guards officer wrote:

"Two squads of about 110 men should be ready to join their battalion in about three week's time. I can safely say that no finer squads will leave this depot for a very long time to come."

In November 1914, ***The Herald*** reported:

"The guard of honour for His Majesty the King at the opening of Parliament will be found by the Scots Guards. The finest men of the battalion are always selected for such duty, and on this occasion the guard will be mainly composed of police from Glasgow and other Scottish towns, who have lately enlisted in the regiment, and are an exceptionally fine body of men."

In May 1915, Glasgow's chief constable prohibited further enlistment except in special circumstances. But by the autumn of 1915, 599 men - almost a third of the Glasgow force - had joined up. By the end of 1915, 692 were in the ranks - of whom 40 had already been killed, with 26 reported missing.

By Armistice Day 1918, 748 Glasgow officers had served in the armed forces - with 112 reported killed or missing presumed dead. Decorations included the UK's only WW1 Victoria Cross awarded to a police officer, 7 Distinguished Conduct Medals, 16 Military Medals, one Meritorious Service Medal, and one Italian Bronze Medal for Valour.

Twenty-three police officers held commissioned rank. A bronze tablet in Glasgow Cathedral, dedicated to Glasgow police officers killed in WW1, was unveiled in 1921.

The Victoria Cross of which a replica is displayed in the museum was won by Sergeant John McAulay - one of five Scots Guards who were awarded the VC during WW1.

A former miner, McAulay - described as an efficient officer and accomplished heavyweight boxer - volunteered on the outbreak of war. In June 1916, while serving with the 1st Battalion, Scots Guards, he was awarded the Distinguished Conduct Medal.

During the Second Battle of Cambrai in 1918, McAulay's three company officers became casualties. His citation for the VC reads:

"For conspicuous bravery and initiative in attack. When all his officers had become casualties, Sergeant McAulay assumed command of the company, and, under shell and machine gun fire, successfully held and consolidated the objective gained. He reorganised the company and cheered on and encouraged his men, and, under heavy fire at close quarters, showed utter disregard of danger.

"Noticing a counter-attack developing on his exposed left flank, he successfully repulsed it by the skilful and bold use of machine guns, aided by two men only, causing heavy enemy casualties.

"Sergeant McAulay also carried his company commander, who was mortally wounded, a long distance to a place of safety under very heavy fire. Twice he was knocked down by the concussion of a bursting shell, but nothing daunted, continued on his way until his objective was achieved, killing two of the enemy who endeavoured to intercept him. Throughout the day this very gallant non-commissioned officer displayed the highest courage, tactical skill, and coolness under exceptionally trying circumstances."

Sgt. John McAulay's VC

Temporary and special constables - recruited from men too old for military service - guarded installations such as bridges, gasworks, tunnels and water works. Anti-German hysteria led to incidents of vandalism. By late 1914, more than 10,000 enemy aliens were interned in the UK.

In 1916, Scotland's Inspector of Constabulary wrote:

"Small burghs cannot protect themselves in times of emergency, and other police authorities are not always able to assist in this way. Small counties could join with large ones. Those already joined under one chief constable have proved the advantage of the system."

In 1915, the Defence of the Realm Act - "DORA" - outlawed keeping of carrier pigeons without a permit, banned Guy Fawkes Night bonfires (a fuel-saving measure), and made it illegal for women afflicted with sexually transmitted diseases to have intercourse with servicemen. Feminists complained bitterly that it was not illegal for infected soldiers to have intercourse with women.

In 1915, Prime Minister David Lloyd George proclaimed:

"We are fighting Germans, Austrians and Drink, and so far as I can see the greatest of these deadly foes is Drink."

DORA restricted hours at pubs near shipyards and munitions plants - leading to a renaissance in shebeening. By 1918, Queen Street, in Glasgow's Govan district - a major shipbuilding area - was described as "the home of shebeens".

Wartime fears and uncertainties encouraged fortune tellers, whose activities were illegal. Police officers regularly arrested such charlatans. They also charged citizens who infringed lighting restrictions. In 1916, a Glasgow youth was convicted of "misusing an electric torch by flashing it at night in College Street, Glasgow". There were fears that German Zeppelin airships would reach the West of Scotland. They had already bombed parts of Edinburgh and appeared over the North-east Scotland.

DORA created an offence of spreading reports "likely to cause disaffection or alarm". In 1916, a Glasgow youth received a month's imprisonment with hard labour for distributing a socialist leaflet. In 1918, police in Glasgow banned the city's socialist brass band from playing in the streets. Teacher and revolutionary John MacLean, described as "the Russian Bolshevik Consul in Glasgow", was jailed at the High Court in Edinburgh on charges of sedition. MacLean had declared:

"The workers, when they rise for their own, are more dangerous to you than the German armies at your gates".

Other charges included "advising munitions workers to ca' canny and to restrict output of munitions".

In 1915, under the Munitions of War Act, 31 Glasgow coppersmiths were fined for going on strike. In 1916, women strikers at a Glasgow brickworks were warned that "any stoppage of work during the war was liable to a penalty of £5 a day". During WW1, police officers also had to inspect hotel registers in which travellers had to list personal details including nationality and business reasons for being in a particular area.

Food rationing began in 1918. Shopkeepers could be fined for selling food above prescribed prices and consumers for wasting food.

There were lighter moments. In 1916, *The Herald* reported:

"Experiments are being made by the police in Glasgow with a new and interesting method for regulation of street vehicular traffic at night. At two of the most crowded crossings in the central district of the city the constables are provided with helmets to which are attached small electric lamps, controlled by a battery carried in the coat pocket. The lamps show the position of the constable and indicate to which of the lines of traffic the crossing is clear."

On the eve of WW2, constables wearing blue-painted steel helmets patrolled streets, with gas masks at the ready. For further protection against possible gas attacks, officers had oilskin coats and trousers and rubber boots. Rattles were to be used to warn the public of gas attacks. Police operated air raid sirens. Police stations were protected by walls of sandbags.

Lighting restrictions - known as the "blackout" - began with the outbreak of war on September 3, 1939 and throughout the war there were many prosecutions for breach of such regulations.

In the first twelve months of the war, there were many prosecutions for offences against "morale", mainly involving pacifists, fascists and communists - but also drunks and eccentrics. In 1939, two young Scottish nationalists in Glasgow were charged with tearing down a recruiting poster. Many of those who fell foul of DORA were well intentioned - or cranks.

In May 1940, a Maryhill man gave a Nazi salute in a barber's shop and shouted: "Heil Hitler - to hell with Britain." He was charged with "having endeavoured to influence public opinion in a manner likely to be prejudicial to the defence of the realm and the efficient prosecution of the war".

In June 1940, Government launched a campaign against "causing alarm and despondency". A Glasgow man who shouted "I am a Nazi spy" in Glasgow's Cumbernauld Road was fined £2.

Fear of "fifth columnists" - Nazi sympathisers who might engage in subversion or sabotage - grew in proportion to Hitler's victories. In May 1940, after the Home Office ordered temporary internment of male Germans and Austrians between the ages of 16 and 60, Glasgow CID launched dawn raids on the homes of "enemy aliens". When the Home Office issued an order for the internment of women aliens, more than 20 German and Austrian women were rounded up in Glasgow. When Italy entered the war in June 1940, many Italians were also arrested. Though many internees were later released, they were subject to curfew and forbidden to enter protected areas such as war factories. "A refugee from Nazi oppression" was arrested when he entered a Paisley factory to sell stationery and other articles. He was admonished.

Within hours of Italy's declaration of war, Italian-owned restaurants, shops and cafes were attacked. In Glasgow's Garscube Road, police tried to keep order when a mob gathered outside an Italian cafe. Despite police efforts, the cafe was wrecked. Similar incidents were reported throughout the city. Italian-owned premises in Largs, Stevenston, Saltcoats, Motherwell, Hamilton and Burnbank were also attacked. In Port Glasgow, crowds smashed windows and looted shops. Police made two baton charges and several arrests were made.

In Hamilton and Burnbank, most offenders were charged with smashing windows. Others were charged with stealing cigarettes and confectionery. Anti-Italian feeling offered golden opportunities for vandalism and looting.

Also in June 1940, six prominent Scottish members of the British Union of Fascists were taken into custody under "Regulation 18b". Aliens were confined to their places of residence between 10.30pm and 6am.

After the fall of France and Belgium, a stream of volunteers presented themselves at police stations to enrol in the hastily formed Local Defence Volunteers - later renamed the Home Guard. Nicknamed "parashots", they were supposed to watch out for Nazi paratroopers. With invasion looming, armed police guarded police stations, gas and electricity plants, and dock gates. Conscientious objectors were not humiliated as in WW1. COs granted conditional exemption, provided they worked in farming or forestry, risked jail if they refused to comply.

As "total war" developed, the UK went much further than Nazi Germany in conscripting both male and female labour. In 1943, at Greenock Sheriff Court, an apprentice driller was jailed for 40 days for absenteeism. At Paisley Sheriff Court, a young man was fined £20 for absenteeism and persistent lateness. Courts fined people who refused certain types of war work. In 1941, after fire-watching became compulsory in workplaces, 27 employees of Glasgow's Copelawhill tram works were fined £1 or seven days' imprisonment for failing to do fire duty.

There was a funny side. After a noisy party in a shelter in Glasgow's East End, teenage boys and girls were arrested for breach of the peace. A magistrate told them:

"You must not turn the shelters into music halls."

As WW2 progressed, millions worked long shifts in war industries, often under threat of enemy air bombardment. All but essential commodities vanished from shops. Police had to deal with attempts to evade increasingly stringent rationing regulations.

In 1941, a Paisley grocer who supplied two customers with extra bacon, butter and tea was fined £5 with the option of 20 days' imprisonment. Rationing of goods such as cigarettes, sweets, ladies' stockings and underwear made illegal trading - the so-called "black market" - acceptable to otherwise law-abiding citizens. The illegal trade was supplied by thieves - amateur and professional.

From 1942, clothing rationing allowed a man to buy a pullover once every five years and a pair of trousers every two years. Clothing restrictions were resented by people earning high wages in war industries. At the lower end of illegal trading, small shopkeepers received stolen cigarettes and slipped regular customers extra supplies "under the counter". By 1940, Glasgow suffered "an epidemic of silk-stocking thefts by women shoplifters".

In 1942, to save paper, Glasgow stores ceased wrapping purchases - resulting in increased shoplifting.

In 1941, a young man was jailed for stealing 10,200 cigarettes from a lorry in Glasgow's Queen Street. A Cambuslang youth was fined £3 or 15 days for stealing eggs from a farm. A Glasgow firm which sold eggs above permitted maximum price was fined £100. In 1943, an up-market Glasgow outfitter sold a school blazer badge at several times the permitted maximum price - and was fined £15.

In 1943, a Glasgow stockeeper sold suit-lengths of cloth to friends without coupons and was jailed for six months. In 1944, a Glasgow company director received three months' imprisonment for resetting 300 pairs of Army-issue khaki panties.

In 1941, a man was jailed for nine months after advertising in newspapers that he had cigarettes and chocolate for sale - payment in advance. The fraud netted him £343. Professional thieves hijacked unattended lorries laden with food, which they sold to unscrupulous shopkeepers willing to buy unrationed items at cut prices.

In 1943, two Largs lorry drivers stole 536 lbs of sugar - representing an individual allowance for 20 years - and were each fined £20. A Glasgow fiscal commented on the seriousness of "inside" jobs on the railways, after three railway workers appeared on charges of stealing whisky, cigarettes and razor blades.

Lacking identity cards and ration books, deserters from the armed forces stole to survive.

In 1943, at Glasgow Sheriff Court, a deserter received 18 months' imprisonment for breaking into houses and stealing clothes, cosmetics, liquor and jewellery - which were sold in dance halls. Also in 1943, an Army deserter was convicted at Glasgow Sheriff Court of stealing 40 rings from 19 jewellers' premises. He was arrested after showing false ID to a police officer.

Between September 1939 and May 1940, 2000 Glaswegians claimed to have lost their ration books and applied for replacements. There was growing illicit demand for such documents. Thieves and forgers stole or replicated identity cards, ration books and clothing and petrol coupons. Coupons were easier to fake than banknotes.

With drink in short supply, thieves filled the gap. In 1942, a shebeen in Glasgow's Gorbals was:

"so well known that practically every Polish seaman who came to the city knew to go there for whisky or wine".

The shebeener was fined £25 or 60 days' imprisonment. In 1944, a Glasgow man was jailed for two years for stealing 400 gallons of whisky from a railway goods yard.

Many police officers were Army reservists and left to resume military service. Many others volunteered for the armed forces. In 1939, the City of Glasgow Police recruited a reserve of 350 ex-police officers. Also in 1939, a second reserve force, the Police War Reserve, was created. In 1941, Government allowed police forces outwith London to recruit 19-year-old men as an alternative to military service.

The City of Glasgow Police advertised for 100 such recruits - who had to be at least 5' 10" in their bare feet. Special constables were again recruited from men too old for military service. War Reserve officers and full-time special constables were exempt from military service over the age of 30.

In March 1941, policing in Motherwell and Wishaw was entrusted to special constables. The experiment was described as successful.

In May 1940, there were in the whole of Scotland only 37 policewomen, two of them sergeants. In that year, the City of Glasgow Police recruited 15 young women and announced:

"More women will be recruited if the experiment is a success."

When the wartime Women's Auxiliary Police Corps was formed, Wishaw town council agreed to establish a corps strength of 16, while Glasgow recruited 220. Corps members became car drivers, wireless and telephone operators, clerical workers and canteen staff. In 1945, Ms Euphemia Mackay - at 5' 1" Glasgow's smallest policewoman - arrested a 20-year-old man who'd tried to steal an army lorry in the city centre.

Wartime lighting restrictions also created new problems for policing in Strathclyde - although an immediately expected "crime wave" failed to materialise.

In 1940, newspapers reported:

"Window-smashing in Greenock housing schemes has become more pronounced since introduction of the black-out".

Glasgow officers were ordered to take "vigorous action" against householders "who do not strictly observe black-out regulations". A number of Dumbarton householders who infringed lighting regulations were each fined £2, with the alternative of 20 days' imprisonment. In Hamilton, a bus driver was fined £4 for driving a bus at 40mph in a built-up area during the "black-out". In 1942, two soldiers committed a "grab and run" at a tearoom in Glasgow's Sauchiehall Street, escaping with £47 under cover of the "black-out".

Also in 1942, youth and welfare organisations discussed "how to combat vice in Glasgow". Alleged problems included "prevalence of loitering by young girls in the city after black-out". In 1943, Glasgow's chief constable claimed "undesirable characters often mix with the customers" at coffee stalls in darkened streets. By 1944, it was reported that housebreakings in Glasgow were seriously increasing "probably due to black-out conditions and scarcity of clothing".

The "Myth of the Blitz" has a special place in WW2 history. Ignoble aspects of human behaviour during the days when "Britain stood alone" have been played down. Police were more familiar with reality - looters who stole from bombed houses and shops and vandals who wrecked air raid shelters. After the devastating Luftwaffe attack on Clydebank on March 13 and 14 1941, 33% of houses in the burgh were so badly damaged they had to be demolished. Another 43% were unfit for habitation.

In the aftermath of such raids, many instances of looting were reported. Looting was regarded as a very serious offence. Culprits were indicted in the High Court. Under DORA, convicted looters could be sentenced to death or penal servitude for life. In practice, draconian penalties were avoided.

In 1941, jail sentences ranging from 18 months to two years were imposed on three men who looted damaged houses in Clydebank. At the High Court in Edinburgh, jail sentences of six months, three months and one month were imposed on Clydeside looters, one of whom had stolen three packets of soap powder from the window of a blitzed shop.

In 1943, "black-out saboteurs" had inflicted so much damage on Greenock air raid shelters that the corporation refused to spend further money on repairs. Doors and seats had been destroyed and shelters made uninhabitable with faeces.

Constable Archibald Walker and Sergeant John MacLeod were awarded the George Medal for acts of bravery in Clydebank. Constables Joseph Park and John Stirling risked their lives to save a three-year-old girl trapped by the foot in a bombed tenement. The official report stated:

"With complete indifference to their personal safety the men worked until the child was extricated five hours later."

Park and Stirling were awarded British Empire Medals. Park's medal is in the museum. Constable Charles Hendry received an OBE.

War Reserve officer Frederick Clark was among many raid victims rescued from bombed buildings in Clydebank. He had been trapped for seven days and died shortly after being freed from the wreckage. One special constable was so badly affected by blast from a bomb which landed beside him that two days later he reported for duty at police HQ in Carlisle - with no memory of how he got there.

Police had to organise identification of dead air raid victims, many of whom were badly mutilated.

In air raids on Clydeside, one War Reserve constable and seven special constables lost their lives. Three hundred and thirty nine members of the City of Glasgow Police served in WW2 - of whom 30 died. Ten officers were decorated or mentioned in dispatches.☐

THE HOT SEAT

MONG portraits of chief constables displayed in Strathclyde Police Museum are James Smart and Percy Sillitoe - two of the most notable holders of that office with the City of Glasgow Police.

Effectively a century apart, James Smart and Percy Sillitoe oversaw technological innovations - and occupied the policing hot seat during times of upheaval and change in the West of Scotland.

In 1862, James Smart became the first senior officer in Strathclyde to bear the title of chief constable. He became Glasgow's superintendent of police in December 1848, inheriting a force of 523 men, including 16 detectives.

Chief Constable James Smart

On March 7, 1848, when Chartist-influenced rioters caused massive disorder in Glasgow, Smart was assistant superintendent in charge of the city's Eastern Division.

As rioters moved through Bridgeton, they cried "Vive la republique!" - an echo of the revolution which had convulsed France in February 1848. Smart had only a few police officers, some special constables, and a handful of Army pensioners. Despite a hail of stones and bricks, this tiny force charged the rioters. But the mob forced Smart's men to retreat into John Street. At the junction of John Street and Main Street, Smart's officers turned to face the rioters. When one of the Army pensioners was injured by a stone, Smart dashed into the crowd, and arrested the culprit.

The mob continued to menace the officers. The pensioners opened fire - killing one demonstrator and mortally wounding others.

84

Some sections of public opinion considered the bloody price worth paying. The conservative *Glasgow Courier* wrote:

"It was a dire necessity. Five minutes longer, and the men of the veterans' battalion would have been disarmed, and had their brains beaten out by their own guns. The discharge of musketry stopped the riots. Otherwise they might have led to the destruction of property of immense value and perhaps the loss of hundreds of lives."

In Smart's 1870 obituary, *The Glasgow Weekly Herald* commented:

"The part which Mr Smart had taken in quelling the disturbances subjected him for a time to no little reproach, but when the feeling of the hour subsided it was seen and acknowledged that his firmness had prevented the riot from attaining even more formidable proportions."

Smart began working life as a traveller in the tea trade. He then became a constable in the Metropolitan Police. After several years in London, he returned to Glasgow and in 1831 joined the Gorbals force, rising to the rank of lieutenant.

In 1835, he was appointed assistant superintendent of Calton Burgh Police. In 1846, Glasgow absorbed the Calton, Gorbals and Anderston forces.

During Smart's period in office, Glasgow expanded dramatically. By 1870, grand terraces and villas lined Great Western Road, the city's *via triumphalis*. Between 1841 and 1871, the population grew from 274,533 to 477,732.

Threat of cholera epidemics receded with supply of fresh water from Loch Katrine - one of the 19th century's most successful examples of "municipal socialism". The 1862 Police Act created a sanitary department in Glasgow - and gave the corporation powers to control overcrowding of houses. In working class tenements, metal plates known as "tickets" were fixed to door frames of flats, stating cubic capacities and permitted number of occupants. Each adult was allowed 300 cubic feet. By 1864, there were 3500 ticketed houses in Glasgow. Police had to inspect ticketed premises, along with common lodging houses. Such duties were resented deeply by working class Glaswegians.

In 1853, when pro-temperance legislation closed pubs on Sundays and limited opening hours, police had to enforce the new laws and root out shebeens.

Smart had to police the burgeoning city within the limitations of Victorian *laissez faire*. The state did not relieve poverty or unemployment. Charities ran soup kitchens, night shelters, homes for "reclaimed females", and "ragged schools" for destitute children - but could not abolish widespread social distress.

Visitors to mid-Victorian Glasgow were horrified by fever-ridden closes, tightly packed with near-destitute families. Sectarian tensions flourished. One observer wrote of the city's Briggait area, where Catholic and Protestant Irish immigrants lived cheek by jowl:

"A row can be got up here in almost no time, especially on a Saturday night, and accordingly policemen are then stationed in it as thick as blackberries."

From the 1860s, Glasgow Corporation began to demolish disease-ridden "rookeries" and erect "model tenements for artisans". Calton's most notorious rookery was "Whisky Close", near present-day Bain Street. It housed 70 familes. Slum clearance left many people homeless - adding to Smart's problems.

Victorian police officers have been described as "domestic missionaries". Officers had to enforce Sabbath observance. In 1850, an Anderston man was fined 10/- for playing pitch and toss on a Sunday. Police also had to break up bare-knuckle prize-fights. In 1868, Peter McGuire was fined three guineas for "having fought a pitched battle with Michael Rody, in the presence of 500 Glasgow roughs". Officers also had to deal with cock-fighting, dog fights and badger-baiting. Bystanders sided with lawbreakers. The last of the "Anderston fighting men" were still at it in the early 1960s.

Smart's period in office coincided with the introduction of two important aids to policing - the electric telegraph and photography. He was chief constable during the trial of Madeleine Smith, the conviction and execution of Dr Edward Pritchard, charged with poisoning his wife and mother-in-law and the last man to be hanged publicly in Glasgow, and the conviction of forger John Henry Greatrex.

James Smart died in 1870, after just under 40 years' police service. He is buried in Glasgow's Southern Necropolis. Officers subscribed for a marble bust of Smart, formally handed over to the Lord Provost in November 1870. Smart's successor, Alexander McCall, said:

"At his death he left the police force of the city in a state of organisation and efficiency inferior to none in the kingdom."

Percy Joseph Sillitoe also took command of the City of Glasgow Police at a time of social unrest and economic downturn. In 1931, when Sillitoe arrived in Glasgow, traditional Clydeside industries such as shipbuilding were in crisis - and remained depressed until rearmament quickened at the end of the decade. The hated means test angered and alienated many thousands of unemployed people.

Sillitoe began his career in colonial police forces in South Africa and Zimbabwe (then known as Rhodesia). In 1920, he was appointed chief constable of Chesterfield, Derbyshire. From there, he went to the East Riding of Yorkshire - and from the outset he was a reforming chief constable. His patch contained the seaside resort of Bridlington, where police had to deal with sexual offences such as indecent exposure. Sillitoe appointed a policewoman to handle such duties, arguing that female complainers would relate more readily to a same-sex officer.

In 1926, Sillitoe became chief constable of Sheffield - then dubbed "Little Chicago" and in the grip of warring gangster factions. Sillitoe earned a reputation as a "gang buster". But he was also an innovator. He reduced the number of divisions in Sheffield - and introduced police boxes, fingerprinting and a forensic laboratory. The latter predated Scotland Yard's facility by at least a year. Sillitoe upgraded living and working conditions for his officers and introduced recreational facilities.

Newspapers began to call Sillitoe:

"The man who smashed the razor gangs, the gang buster of Sheffield".

With those credentials, Sillitoe, aged 43, took command of the City of Glasgow Police - the UK's second-largest force. There can be little doubt that his gang-busting reputation was one of the key factors in Glasgow Corporation's decision to appoint him.
Sillitoe immediately began reforming the Glasgow force. Divisions were reduced from 11 to seven, 13 police stations were closed. The city's beat system was transformed by introduction of a city-wide network of police boxes linking beat officers with divisional HQs.

Chief Constable Sir Percy Sillitoe

Sillitoe abolished many middle and senior ranks and introduced compulsory retirement for officers after 30 years' service. He established fingerprinting and photographic bureaux. In April 1932, Glasgow CID officers identified their first offender by fingerprinting. Sillitoe also employed female civilians as telephonists, typists and clerks, replacing police officers in such roles.

Soon after appointment, Sillitoe visited the USA, where he noted technical and scientific aids to policing, such as lie detectors and radio-equipped vehicles. First demonstration of police radio in Glasgow took place in November 1932. Sillitoe announced that the city would thenceforth be divided into patrol areas, each served by a radio-equipped police vehicle. By 1936, Glasgow had 29 radio-equipped police vehicles. One councillor described radio cars as "mechanism gone mad".

So-called "motor bandits" were in the headlines. Yet when Sillitoe took office, the City of Glasgow Police had only five vans and four cars. "Motor bandits" had a head start on officers compelled to travel on foot, by bicycle - or in tramcars. By the mid-1930s, Sillitoe had equipped his force with a fleet of sleek Alvis Speed Twenty patrol cars.

Sillitoe was aware of close links between crime and deprivation. As the Great Depression worsened, young people went from school to the dole queues. While conscientiously avoiding party politics, Sillitoe observed:

"There can be little doubt that the increase of crime in the city is due in some measure to the difficult times through which we are passing, and that unemployment is the main factor, especially in the case of crimes involving the disappropriation of property."

Supportive of social work approaches, Sillitoe agreed, in 1933, to address unemployed people in a Partick cinema. With hindsight, his lecture topic seems somewhat arcane - "Big Game Hunting in Africa". Sillitoe's reminiscences of shooting bull elephants did not appeal to Partick's jobless inhabitants. He was jeered at and treated to an impromptu rendering of "The Internationale".

Despite hunger marches and mass meetings on Glasgow Green, the city was spared much of the political violence of London and other cities. Clashes between fascists and their opponents were small-scale. But sectarianism flourished. Glasgow's East End was the stamping ground of the "Protestant" Billy Boys, led by notorious thug Billy Fullerton. In the 1990s, a book on Glasgow gangs portrayed Fullerton as a misunderstood working class hero. The same book relentlessly abused Sillitoe as an enemy of working class people. In practice, Fullerton was an extortionist, a provider of "muscle" for illegal moneylenders - and a physical coward. He also dabbled with Sir Oswald Mosley's British Union of Fascists.

Sillitoe knew most Glaswegians loathed Fullerton and his kind. Fullerton once attempted

Homemade gang weapon from Strathclyde Police Museum's collection.

to extort cash from an Italian chip shop owner - who coolly stepped from behind his counter and fractured the gangster's skull with an axe handle. Fullerton and his "team" never entered that shop again.

Fullerton's followers clashed with nominally Roman Catholic rivals, the Norman Conks, led by Bill Bowman. Innocent pedestrians were often frightened and injured during such encounters. There is actually little hard evidence that Glasgow was particularly infested with "Razor Kings". Favourite gang weapons were knives, hatchets, stones and pickshafts.

Sillitoe recruited the so-called "C Division Specials" - an information-gathering network of "irregulars" whose ranks included ex-cons, prostitutes, bar staff - and, famously, Aggie Reid, a former member of the by then defunct Redskins gang.

Improved communications, high-quality intelligence and greater mobility combined with Sillitoe's decisiveness to tackle the gangs. In one incident in 1934, police officers with drawn batons "ambushed" several hundred Billy Boys marching behind a flute band as they headed for battle in a reputedly "Catholic" area.

But fines - often paid by shopkeepers terrorised into paying "protection" - were ineffective deterrents. Sillitoe appealed to the courts to support his campaign. The courts obliged, and neds were sentenced to terms of imprisonment with hard labour.

However hard Sillitoe moved against the gangs, he never fully "bust" them. As late as 1937, despite official claims of "returning prosperity", Glasgow still had more than 87,000 unemployed people - and Fullerton and Bowman retained substantial "private armies".

Also during Sillitoe's term of office, five magistrates were jailed for corruption - including a chairman of the police committee.

Sillitoe continued to make headlines. When he introduced chequered black and white cap bands - now increasingly adopted by police forces worldwide - it was dubbed "the Sillitoe tartan". Reporters suggested Sillitoe's information-gathering tactics were based on methods he'd used in the African bush. Stories had it that he "prowled the streets at night dressed as a workman" - and he was supposed to have attended funerals of poor people found dead with no known relatives and to have used his own money to give meals and drinks to the few strangers who attended such events.

The truth or otherwise of such tales remains to be established. More certainly, Sillitoe expressed admiration for Guy Aldred, anarchist, conscientious objector, pacifist, birth control pioneer and free speech campaigner - Glasgow's famous "knickerbocker politician". Aldred's George Street HQ became a one-person citizen's advice bureau for many of the city's poorest people. Aldred's legal knowledge and eloquence helped poor people challenge slum landlords. Both men seem to have kept their distance, but each seems to have understood that the other was trying to improve the world he found. Aldred's libertarian socialism had no place for Billy Fullerton or Bill Bowman.

Just prior to WW2, the IRA carried out a number of attacks in Glasgow. Sillitoe's "C Division Specials" helped apprehend two male "nuns" in charge of a coffin crammed with small arms and hand grenades.

In 1939, Sillitoe recruited women volunteers for a Women's Auxiliary Police Corps under Bailie Violet Roberton, a popular councillor. The WAPC grew to a force several hundreds strong and took over many mainstream policing duties. Their hats bore the "Sillitoe tartan". In 1942, Sillitoe was knighted - the first Scottish chief constable so honoured.

In 1943, Sillitoe became chief constable of Kent County Constabulary - a Government-

89

inspired merger of nine forces. His new command was part of meticulous preparations for D-Day - the Allied invasion of Hitler's "Fortress Europe". In 1946, Prime Minister Clement Atlee appointed Sillitoe director general of MI5 - a post he held until 1953.
Sillitoe died in 1962. His *Herald* obituary commented:

"During his years in Glasgow he practically revolutionised the police force, and he left it in a state of efficiency and up-to-date organisation such as it had never previously attained."

Smart and Sillitoe faced remarkably similar challenges, to which they responded with decisiveness, administrative competence, willingness to innovate - and restraint. Both acted with force and determination - but also carried public opinion with them. Both men seem to have earned their remarkably similar epitaphs. ☐

PORRIDGE AND PANOPTICONS

STRATHCLYDE Police Museum displays some photographs of damage done to HM Prison, Barlinnie, Glasgow, during riots in the 1980s. Police officers are required to investigate such incidents and to prefer charges where offences have been committed.

Until the 19th century, jailing people was a costly option for small, cash-strapped communities. Minor offenders were usually punished by being whipped by public hangmen. At Inveraray, Argyll, in 1718, Dugald McDugald, convicted of theft, was:

"Whipt with thirty-nine stripes by the hand of the executions and thereafter his right ear to be nailed to the gallowsfoot, there to continue for the space of ane hour."

Whipping was frequently followed by banishment from burghs or counties - with individual offenders free to live elsewhere in the kingdom. In 1773, Malcolm Dunn, banished from Glasgow for resetting stolen goods, was whipped out of town by the hangman - the route was from the Tolbooth along Gallowgate to the city limits.

Felons guilty of serious offences were either executed by public hanging or transported to penal settlements in the colonies. In the 17th and 18th centuries, convicts were shipped to Maryland, Virginia and the Caribbean. When the American War of Independence halted transportation to North America, convicts were dispatched to Australia. Scotland's penal code never contained as many capital offences as England's, and fewer Scots than English were sentenced to death.

Between 1810 and 1821, the Scottish rate of transportation was less than a quarter of that of England, per head of population. Scottish prisoners awaiting transportation were initially conveyed to work in naval dockyards at Chatham, Portsmouth and Woolwich. They were accommodated in old ships or hulks moored offshore. Conditions were appalling. Convict ships sailing to Australia were equally grim. Transportation ended in 1868. The experience featured in 19th-century ballads:

"There wis a lass frae Dundee
Bonnie Jeanie wis her name
Twenty years transported for a-playing o the game
The captain bought her freedom and selt her oot o hand
She gave us all good usage, boys, unto Van Diemen's Land."
"So, come a ye puir o Scotland
That labour and do toil
Yer robbed o every blessing, every product o the soil
Yer prood imperial landlord
Jist disobey his command
He'll send ye on a British hulk tae ploo Van Diemen's Land."

Sometimes, jails in Scotland were self-contained Bridewells or "Houses of Correction". More often, they were incorporated into principal public buildings of towns. Between 1757 and 1820, at Inveraray, Argyll, the Town House, County Courthouse and County Jail were accommodated in a single neo-classical building. The prison was on the ground floor. Prisoners walked:

"in a grated piazza in front of their cells, just in line of the principal street, and exposing the miserable appearance of their apartments and furniture to shock the feelings of every passer-by".

Security was lax. There were so many escapes from the building that townspeople took turns at guard duty. Glasgow's Tolbooth jail seems to have been equally insecure. Petty offenders could avoid detention for non-payment of fines by leaving articles in pledge. In 1821, two men fined for fighting at Calton Burgh Police Court, Glasgow, escaped imprisonment by leaving three yards of blue cloth in pledge for 14 days. In 1822, Samuel Jackson, sentenced to 14 days at Calton Burgh Police Court, tholed his assize by whitewashing the police office and painting a superintendent's room.

As late as 1805, Kilmarnock's new council chambers contained cells, described as "low-roofed, almost without light or air". But new penal concepts were coming into vogue. One of the first custom-built jails - designed on the "Panopticon Principle", allowing warders constant sight of prisoners - was Edinburgh's Bridewell, built in 1791-95.

In 1807, the jail attached to Glasgow's Tolbooth had only 32 cells. In 1814, a new courthouse and prison opened on a new site facing Glasgow Green. It had facilities for "air and exercise", water closets in every gallery, and an infirmary. Debtors had better facilities than criminal prisoners. A visitor in 1818 was not impressed:

"I never witnessed a more melancholy spectacle. Idleness, clamour and dissipation prevailed on every side, and when we first entered the prison, the mixed din of fiddling, laughing, and riotous vociferation, was truly appalling."

After demolition of the jail, the site continued to be known as Jail Square, until civic leaders rechristened it Jocelyn Square - the name it retains today.

Penal reformers dubbed prisons "nurseries of vice" - with juvenile offenders thrown among hardened criminals who tutored them in crime. As a result, reformatories opened in many towns. By 1850, Glasgow had a House of Refuge for young offenders, but some children preferred prison. Newspapers reported a little Glasgow boy - "so diminutive his head could not be seen above the bar" - who was convicted of theft and offered the alternatives of prison or the House of Refuge. He chose prison. In 1862, inmates rioted in the House of Refuge, "breaking every pane of glass within their reach". Police arrested 11 ringleaders. By the mid-1800s, reformers had changed the prison landscape. Scotland's jails no longer echoed to the sounds of "fiddling, laughing, and riotous vociferation".

Prior to 1839, when a Board of Directors of Scottish Prisons was set up, the jails were administered by royal burghs. The board reduced greatly the number of prisons in Scotland

and established county prison boards. The Scottish board aimed to give each county one main prison. Within 10 years, the number of prisons was halved from 170 to 85. Jails were to operate the "separate system" - ensuring minimum contact between inmates.

Under the separate system, inmates were isolated in individual cells. Women were segregated from men, juveniles from adults. It was thought criminals could be reformed - with the help of solitude, prayer, and frequent visits from chaplains - if they were kept from bad influences such as habitual offenders. Communication between prisoners was forbidden - even during exercise periods. Some prison authorities even insisted inmates wore face masks. Isolation aimed to break a prisoner's spirit - supposedly a necessary preliminary to repentance.

Glasgow's Duke Street prison was built in the 1820s on the site of an older Bridewell accommodating vagrants and prostitutes. When Barlinnie prison opened in 1882, Duke Street became largely a women's prison. In 1866, a reporter from the *Glasgow Weekly Herald* visited Duke Street prison - which then held between 400 and 500 male and female prisoners, most of them held under the "separate system":

"When a visitor enters a cell, the inmate, if he is seated, starts to his feet, doffs his cap, and stands in a humble posture until the door is once more closed upon him. When we entered the kitchen where a number of prisoners were at dinner, they instantly laid down their spoons, ranked themselves in line, and stood meek as abject menials until we turned our backs upon them, when dinner was once more resumed."

The separate system even operated in the prison chapel:

"A passage separates the pulpit from the congregation, and over all the seats there is an iron grating to keep the prisoners from communicating with one another. Each seat is separated from the next in order, and three officers are perched up aloft to watch the movements of the worshippers."

Some prisoners worked at their own trades, such as tailoring, baking and shoemaking. Women prisoners knitted, laundered and sewed. Prisoners sentenced to hard labour teased oakum - unravelling fibres from short lengths of old rope, used to caulk the seams of wooden ships.

Other prisoners were assigned to crank machines:

"These machines are not unlike fat grindstones, with a stout handle sticking out from the side. One is placed within every cell where the hard labour is to be performed, and fixed against the wall next the passage, where a little dial, communicating with the machine inside, shows without fail every turn of the weary handle. There can be no shamming, therefore, on the part of the prisoners, for each moment's idleness or laziness is recorded like clockwork, and if the allocated task is not accomplished there will be a scarcity of rations, and no mistake."

Warders could tighten screws on cranks, making them harder to turn - the origin of the term "screw" for a prison officer. At Inveraray's new model prison, opened in 1848, prisoners had to clock up 14,400 revolutions of the crank per day.

Photo: Ian Sutherland

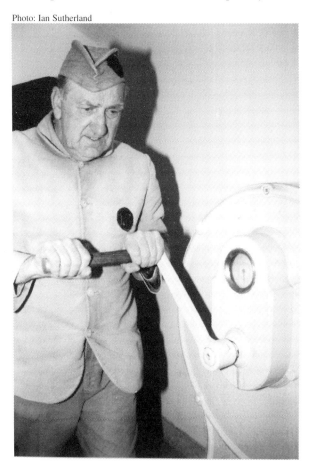

A 19th-century prison crank being used by an "inmate" at Inveraray Jail Museum.

At Duke Street prison, teasing and turning was varied by daily turns in an exercise ground known as "the iron cage" - described as "shaped something like an old-fashioned circular mousetrap". The cage was divided into compartments by walls running towards the centre of the circle. The roof and sides were composed of iron bars. Each prisoner had half an hour's exercise per day:

"A warder sits up aloft in a sort of rostrum, where he can see everything that passes below".

Condemned cells in each block were segregated by iron gates. When prisoners were awaiting execution, the gates were guarded night and day.

Every male prisoner had a cell to himself. Women were sometimes accommodated two or three to a cell - a slight relaxation of the solitary system. Debtors had:

"a common hall where they pass the most of their time reading, discussing things in general, and playing practical jokes".

Photo: Ian Sutherland

Oakum-picking at Inveraray Jail Museum. Meaningless repetitive work served the apparently contradictory penal aims of "uplifting" and "punishing".

Redemption and reform ran side by side with punishment. Inveraray's prison library contained volumes such as *Christian Philosophy, Christian Biography, Christian Instructions*, and *The Parables Explained.*

Small local jails were expensive to run. In 1839, there were 178 locally administered prisons in Scotland. By 1888, only 15 remained. The state took over.

Scotland now (1998) has 19 prisons, remand centres and young offenders institutions. Cornton Vale, near Stirling, is Scotland's only female prison.

By the 1960s, issues such as alleged brutality by prison staff, serious overcrowding, and insanitary and depressing conditions began to make headlines. Serious disturbances broke out in many Scottish jails - with TV cameras focusing on dramatic rooftop protests. There were distressing incidents of hostage-taking.

Central government commenced major programmes of refurbishment and new building. When the West of Scotland's newest prison, at Shotts, Lanarkshire, was opened in 1987, politicians expressed the hope that greatly improved living conditions would eliminate sources of prison discontent. But within months, Shotts too was embroiled in destructive and violent "prison riots".

In the past, tobacco was the "currency" of prison life. In the late-20th century, it has been repeatedly alleged that drugs have taken over that role - with "dope kings" replacing "tobacco barons" in Scottish prisons.

Supporters of "law and order" demand increasingly longer sentences and tougher prison regimes. Reformers seek greater emphasis on improved opportunities for personal development, education and training - along with expansion of alternatives to prison, such as community service programmes. But for all their emphasis on pointless "make work" schemes such as cranks and treadmills, along with silence and solitary confinement, past generations were not unaware of wider issues.

In 1912, a Glasgow prison doctor wrote:

"One thing visitors cannot miss seeing, yet do not observe, though it is of much more significance than the cleanliness they admire: the good temper and tractability of the prisoners."

"These people are sent to prison because they cannot obey the law, but while in prison they are not rebellious; so that it is reasonable to infer that there has been something in the conditions of their life outside which has led them into misconduct, and not that they are inherently incapable of behaving themselves."□